The food & cooking of
ROMANIA & BULGARIA

The food & cooking of
ROMANIA &
BULGARIA

traditions • ingredients • tastes • over 65 recipes • 370 photographs

SILVENA JOHAN LAUTA

Photography by Martin Brigdale

This edition is published by Aquamarine,
an imprint of Anness Publishing Ltd, Hermes House,
88–89 Blackfriars Road, London SE1 8HA;
tel. 020 7401 2077; fax 020 7633 9499

www.aquamarinebooks.com; www.annesspublishing.com

If you like the images in this book and would like to
investigate using them for publishing, promotions
or advertising, please visit our website
www.practicalpictures.com for more information.

UK distributor: Book Trade Services; tel. 0116 2759086;
fax 0116 2759090; uksales@booktradeservices.com;
exportsales@booktradeservices.com

Australian distributor: Pan Macmillan Australia;
tel. 1300 135 113; fax 1300 135 103;
customer.service@macmillan.com.au

New Zealand distributor: David Bateman Ltd;
tel. (09) 415 7664; fax (09) 415 8892

Publisher: Joanna Lorenz
Editorial Director: Helen Sudell
Project Editor: Emma Clegg
Designer: Lisa Tai
Illustrator: Rob Highton
Photography: Martin Brigdale
Food Stylist: Fergal Connolly
Prop Stylist: Helen Trent
Romanian translator: Costel Buterchi
Proofreading Manager: Lindsay Zamponi
Production Controller: Wendy Lawson

© Anness Publishing Ltd 2010

ETHICAL TRADING POLICY

Because of our ongoing ecological investment
programme, you, as our customer, can have the
pleasure and reassurance of knowing that a tree is
being cultivated on your behalf to naturally replace
the materials used to make the book you are holding.
For further information about this scheme, go to
www.annesspublishing.com/trees

Front cover shows Red Pepper Bürek;
for recipe, see page 41.

PUBLISHER'S NOTES

Although the advice and information in this book are
believed to be accurate and true at the time of going to
press, neither the author nor the publisher can accept any
legal responsibility or liability for any errors or omissions
that may be made nor for any inaccuracies nor for any
harm or injury that comes about from following
instructions or advice in this book.

- Bracketed terms are intended for American readers.
- For all recipes, quantities are given in both metric and
  imperial measures and, where appropriate, in standard
  cups and spoons. Follow one set of measures, but not a
  mixture, because they are not interchangeable.
- Standard spoon and cup measures are level.
  1 tsp = 5ml, 1 tbsp = 15ml, 1 cup = 250ml/8fl oz.
- Australian standard tablespoons are 20ml. Australian
  readers should use 3 tsp in place of 1 tbsp for measuring
  small quantities of gelatine, flour, salt, etc.
- American pints are 16fl oz/2 cups. American readers
  should use 20fl oz/2½ cups in place of 1 pint when
  measuring liquids.
- Electric oven temperatures in this book are for
  conventional ovens. When using a fan oven, the
  temperature will probably need to be reduced by about
  10–20°C/20–40°F. Since ovens vary, you should check
  with your manufacturer's instruction book for guidance.
- The nutritional analysis given for each recipe is calculated
  per portion (i.e. serving or item), unless otherwise stated.
  If the recipe gives a range, such as Serves 4-6, then the
  nutritional analysis will be for the smaller portion size, i.e.
  6 servings. Measurements for sodium do not include salt
  added to taste.
- Medium (US large) eggs are used unless
  otherwise stated.

Contents

Introduction

Bulgaria and Romania lie next to each other in the far eastern corner of Europe, bordering the Black Sea. Although these two countries have quite different cultures, and even different alphabets – Bulgaria uses the Cyrillic alphabet, like Russia – their rugged landscapes are strikingly similar. The cuisines have much in common, with regional specialities drawn from the produce of the landscape around them, whether plains, hillsides or mountains. The main differences are that Romania is defined by its substantial fare based on meat, root vegetables and beans, whereas the Bulgarian diet has a lighter, more Mediterranean emphasis, due to the sunnier, warmer climate.

The landscapes of Romania and Bulgaria are both dominated by huge mountain ranges that march imposingly across the countryside, their peaks glistening with snow all year round. Both countries also contain crumbling medieval castles and monasteries set in deep forests, far from human habitation, set in a landscape that is home to the last wild wolves and bears of Europe. Between the two countries flows the mighty River Danube, linking them together like a silver thread between the mountains.

The vast waterway of the Danube rises in the alpine region of the Black Forest in Germany and winds through seven other European countries before, in the final stretch of its epic voyage, forming almost the whole of the boundary between Romania and Bulgaria. Northern Bulgaria and southern Romania are the beneficiaries of the mature Danube's gifts: irrigation for crops, drinking water, fishing and transport. The river, with its slow progress to the coast, not only defines the

boundary, but also gives life to the flat plains it has forged over millennia and feeds the economies of both countries.

ROMANIA

This beautiful country with its extensive forests, mountains and lakes is just beginning to shake off the economic and political restrictions that held back its progress in the last century. Tourism is booming, and no wonder: there is much to see. The landscape is a stunning mixture of wild natural habitats and a romantic heritage in the form of ancient churches and castles. Modern industry and the legacy of the years of communism encroach on the cities; however, there is still plenty of untouched countryside, where chamois, stags and wild boar live undisturbed except by hunters looking for game to make a tasty stew.

The Carpathian Mountains

These dramatic mountains stretch through Austria, the Czech Republic, Slovakia, Poland, Ukraine, Romania, Serbia and Montenegro, and northern Hungary. Romania takes up by far the largest area in the south of this mountain range and the climate here can be quite extreme. It is cold enough for good skiing in the winter and hot

LEFT Haystacks and agricultural landscape in the rolling green hills of Budeşti, south-east of Bucharest.

enough for swimming, hiking and walking in the summer. The south-facing lower mountain slopes of central Romania are ideal for growing grapes and hops, as well as the huge crop of plums that are such an everyday feature of Romanian life. Most of these plums find their way into ţuică, the fiery plum brandy served in every bar, café and restaurant, accompanied by pickles or slices of spicy sausage.

The Danube plains
To the south and east of the country the Danube snakes through low-lying plains and marshland on its way to the Black Sea, leaving layers of silt and many freshwater lagoons in its path. This fertile soil has made eastern and southern Romania the breadbasket of the country. Here farmers grow grains for bread and the staple dish of Romania, mămăligă (a kind of polenta), and raise poultry, pigs, cattle and sheep for their meat and dairy products.

The Black Sea wetlands
Spreading out into the Black Sea, the Danube Delta is a famous wetland habitat for native and migratory birds.

ABOVE Fishermen on their way home after a week of fishing in the Danube Delta, Romania.

Keen birdwatchers might see flamingos, wild geese, swans and even pelicans flocking here all the year round, ever ready to dive for the fish that are so plentiful in these warm waters. There are 45 different species of freshwater fish to be found in the Danube Delta region, including carp, pike and trout, many of which end up in a classic Romanian sour fish soup, flavoured with lemon juice or vinegar.

A thrifty cuisine
The climate in Romania varies greatly because of contrasts in its topography. However, the winter weather is very cold over most of the country, so preserving the good things grown in the summer months is a vital part of Romanian cuisine. Dairy products such as yogurt and cheese add flavour and nutritional value to the diet, while pickled vegetables, cured or smoked pork sausage and ham lend their tangy zest to soups and stews.

ABOVE A shepherd from the Făgăraş Mountains, the highest range of the Southern Carpathians in Romania.

Bucharest: the Romanian capital
Built on the Dâmboviţa river, Bucharest was named after Bucur, a mysterious figure in Romanian legend. Throughout its history, many cultures have shaped the buildings and culture of Bucharest, from medieval Christianity, through the orientalism of the Ottoman Empire and the drabness of communism, to a proud new 21st-century nationalism. There are still ancient churches and grand palaces nestling between the shiny skyscraper office blocks and functional apartment buildings needed to house its population of almost 2 million people.

In the late 19th century, Bucharest underwent a facelift, and some beautiful parks and open spaces were created, along with wide boulevards – ideal places for a pleasant stroll. Street stalls and patisseries invite the pedestrian to sample a typical Romanian savoury pastry, and there are plenty of cafés and restaurants serving dishes such as moussaka and baklava, derived from the oriental recipes of the Ottoman Empire.

BULGARIA

The mountain plain that runs across the centre of Bulgaria divides the country into three distinct areas: the low-lying Danube plain to the north, where Bulgaria faces Romania over the Danube River; the high peaks of the Balkan Mountains, stretching in a long ridge from the Black Sea coast to the Serbian border; and the warm Mediterranean climate of southern Bulgaria where it touches northern Greece and Turkey. Despite the differences in temperature between north and south, Bulgarian cuisine tends to resemble the Mediterranean cooking of countries further south, rather than the more solid fare of its northern neighbour, Romania. Bulgarians love to eat plenty of fresh vegetables, especially tomatoes, garlic, cucumber, onions and spices, all of which can be grown locally and preserved in pickled or dried form for the cold winters.

Bulgaria's larder

Northern Bulgaria is dominated, as is southern Romania, by the River Danube. The flat, low-lying plains on each side of

the river are fertile farming country, full of crops of all kinds, especially grains such as wheat, corn and barley. This is also the place to find acres of bright, nodding sunflowers grown for their seeds, a major Bulgarian export. Several major fishing ports lie on the Black Sea coast, although over-fishing

ABOVE Panicata Lake in the valley below the Hajduta peak in the Rila Mountains, Rila National Park, Bulgaria.

of this small, non-tidal sea has caused problems for the industry in recent years. However, fish remains an important part of the Bulgarian diet in the coastal towns and villages, usually served quite plainly grilled or fried to preserve its fresh flavour.

The central region

The high Balkan Mountains and the even higher Rhodope Mountains to the south are a major attraction for tourists looking for ideal skiing conditions in the winter. The mountains also provide plenty of hiking and sporting activities in the summer, with expeditions to see the bears, wolves, wild cats and eagles that still live in these relatively undisturbed regions. Visitors love to sample the traditional food and drink to be found here, particularly the hearty peasant-style dishes based on meat flavoured with local wild mushrooms and herbs, which can satisfy the biggest appetites.

The Bulgarians' favourite alcoholic drink is a very strong brew of plum or grape brandy made from the fruits

BELOW School children helping with the tomato harvest; tomatoes are probably the most significant vegetable crop in Bulgaria.

BELOW The Valley of Roses in Kazanluk, at the foot of the Balkan Mountains, has produced rose oil for generations.

grown on the lower mountain slopes. It is known as rakia, and is similar in taste and strength to Romanian ţuică. They also make tasty, strong beer, and have a world-renowned range of wines.

Mineral springs abound in the central region, forcing their way up through the rocks to overflow down into the valleys. This water is reputed to have wonderful health-giving qualities and has led to the establishment of several spa resorts based on natural springs.

Between the Balkan Mountains and the Rhodope Mountains lies a beautiful valley that grows a very special crop. The Valley of Roses bursts into bloom every May and June, and local people carefully pick each rose by hand, after which they are processed into scented oils for adding to perfumes, chocolates and liqueurs.

The southern hills

The border between Bulgaria and Greece runs along the southern edge of the Rhodope Mountains, and then falls to the lower hills to join Turkey

RIGHT The terrain of Romania and Bulgaria is varied, with mountainous areas, fertile valleys, plains and the Black Sea coastline.

LEFT A man gathering hay on a donkey wagon near Varna, Bulgaria – sunflowers are an important cash crop in this region.

before ending in the Black Sea. This southern area of Bulgaria naturally has a much warmer climate than the mountains and valleys further north. In the sheltered valleys and gentle hills, all sorts of vegetable and fruit crops thrive, particularly tomatoes, which are exported all over the world and used in many of the traditional dishes. The staple salad of Bulgaria, shopska salata, is eaten at almost every meal, and is based on local chopped tomatoes from the southern region, with cucumber, onions, bell peppers and feta, the fragrant white semi-hard cheese made from sheep's milk. Dairy products are plentiful here, especially yogurt, which is a real Bulgarian speciality. The traditional kind is full-fat (whole), very thick and creamy, and is often served stirred into soup or made into a refreshing salty drink for a hot summer's day.

Sofia: the Bulgarian capital

One of the most ancient cities of Europe, settlements have been excavated on the site of Sofia that date back at least 7,000 years. Nowadays, central Sofia is a delightful mixture of ancient churches, castles and ruins, set alongside some rather bleak, large-scale communist-era buildings and thriving new shopping centres.

As the cosmopolitan capital, Sofia generally has a more upmarket and adventurous quality of cuisine. However, traditional fare can still be found in its restaurants, with Turkish and Greek flavours alongside the classic Bulgarian dishes, plus a sprinkling of Western-style fast food.

But the real home of Bulgarian cuisine is on the streets, where stalls and shops offer all kinds of delicacies, such as barbecued corn on the cob; roasted chestnuts; thin pancakes, similar to crêpes; cheese-filled filo pastries known as banitsa; or, for the carnivore, kebabs, meatballs and lukanka (a salami-style sausage) with a glass of rakia.

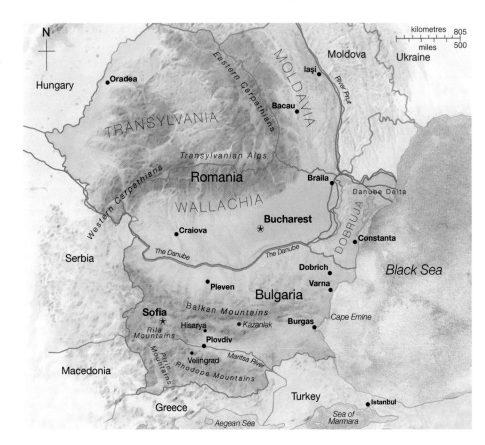

A multifarious history

Despite their background of repeated invasion, the peoples of Romania and Bulgaria have a national spirit and culture to be proud of. The vast and powerful armies of the Roman, Byzantine and Ottoman empires have dominated these smaller countries for hundreds of years, and in the last century both countries became part of the vast communist bloc of eastern Europe – and yet the strong character of each country survives, in its architecture, art, music and cuisine.

Early history

The modern-day territories of Bulgaria and Romania are situated in the ancient lands of Thrace and Dacia. The history of invasion, power transfer and tribal movement is complex in both regions.

The first Bulgarians were Bulgar tribes from the highlands of Siberia and from central Asia who moved down towards Europe, many settling in Thrace. This covered most of modern-day Bulgaria, as well as parts of Greece and Turkey, extending from the Aegean Sea to the Carpathians. The Thracians were the second largest tribe in the ancient world and were renowned as fearsome warriors, but the Romans finally conquered them.

The Kingdom of Dacia included modern Romania and Moldova and parts of Hungary and Bulgaria. The kingdom reached its peak under King Burebista, the first Thracian king and a contemporary of Caesar, who reigned from 82 to 44 BC, but the kingdom was finally conquered by the Romans at the end of the 1st century AD.

Many colonists settled here in different periods. Tribes arriving in Roman times included those from Moesia (now Serbia), Macedonia, Gaul (a race from modern-day northern France and parts of Belgium, Germany and Italy) and Syria. In the 4th century the principle settlers were the Huns (from western China), the Slavs (from west Asia), the Armenians, and the Avars (from Mongolia).

Unity and division

The First Bulgarian Empire was established in the 7th century. Under Tsar Simeon, who ruled from AD 893 to

BELOW A painting showing Wallachian and Moldavian noblemen on horseback in the late 16th century.

927, Bulgaria's Golden Age began, an era of artistic creativity. The first written laws were introduced at this time and Bulgaria became the first Slavic country to adopt Christianity. The next few centuries saw Bulgaria annexed by the Byzantine Empire and a Second Bulgarian Empire and further domination by the Ottoman Empire. This final blow meant that the state became a vassal of the Ottoman Empire for 500 years.

The territory of present-day Romania had formed itself into three distinct principalities by the 13th century: Moldavia, Wallachia and Transylvania. All three were united in 1918 following the end of World War I. Moldavia and Wallachia were influenced by many cultures, but were made up of mostly Romanian people. Situated on the border of the Ottoman Empire, for many years they repelled invasions by the Turks, although they became part of the Ottoman Empire during the 15th and 16th centuries. In both principalities the boyars – members of the aristocracies – ruled with bloody suppression. Vlad the Impaler is an infamous example of one of these tyrants, and he became the main inspiration for Count Dracula in Bram Stoker's novel of 1897.

World wars and communism

In the Balkan Wars, before World War I, Bulgaria lost land to Romania. They later backed the losing side in World War I, leading to more territorial losses. Conversely, Romania gained territory and joined the Allies, so that after the 1918 victory by the Allies, Romanian lands became unified once again during the

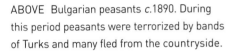

ABOVE Bulgarian peasants c.1890. During this period peasants were terrorized by bands of Turks and many fled from the countryside.

interwar period. World War II saw Romania join the Axis, the countries opposed to the Allies, and by the end of the war the Soviet communists were in occupation and retained control.

The communists also took power in Bulgaria, exiling King Simeon II in 1946. Communist rule lasted, as in Romania, until the 1990s. For most of this period, Todor Zhivkov was the Bulgarian leader, nationalizing industry, collectivizing agriculture and bringing the Orthodox Church under state control. He was removed in 1989, but not so violently as Nicolae Ceauşescu of Romania, who was executed after a popular uprising against the stricter police state.

Democracy and accession to the EU
Since the return of free elections in 1990, Bulgaria has had much economic difficulty and corruption. However, more recently, the economy has been growing steadily with huge investment in the property market, particularly in the Black Sea area. Bulgaria became a member of NATO in 2004 and a full member state

RIGHT Vlad the Impaler, also known as Vlad III and Vlad Dracula, occupied the throne of Wallachia from 1456 to 1476.

of the EU in 2007. Today it is a popular holiday destination in Europe; tourists are attracted to the ski and beach resorts, providing an invaluable source of income.

In Romania, the first government elected in 1990 was accused of being made up of ex-communists. Subsequent anti-communist protests were bloodily suppressed in what became known as the June Mineriad – an event that ruined Romania's image. Since then, Romania has sought to develop closer ties with western Europe and to strengthen its economy to stem the mass emigration of many Romanians to other parts of Europe and the USA. It entered NATO in 2004 and joined the EU in January 2007.

ABOVE Bulgarians welcome back King Simeon II in 1996 after 50 years of exile, after the monarchy was overthrown by a communist coup in 1946. He later served as prime minister.

THE MYTHOLOGY OF DRACULA
The story of *Dracula* was written by Bram Stoker in 1897. The real Dracula, Prince Vlad Dracula, was born in about 1431 in Sighişoara, Transylvania, to the ruler of Wallachia in the south of modern-day Romania. Dracula's father was assassinated and his older brother tortured to death by the Turks and the boyars. In revenge, Dracula began a reign of cruelty, torturing his victims in horrific ways, but his favourite method was impalement, which gave him his nickname, Vlad the Impaler.

In 1462 he raided across the Danube and killed more than 23,000 Turks and Bulgarians. When the Turks arrived at Dracula's stronghold to exact revenge they were confronted by a dreadful sight: rows of fences with impaled Hungarians, Moldavians and Wallachians and people hanging from the tree branches.

All this history would have been known to Stoker and used as inspiration for *Dracula*. His frightening and gripping tale also included the mythology of vampires and the undead, still strong in Eastern Europe during the 19th century.

Traditions & festivals

The two countries of Romania and Bulgaria share such a long history that it is unsurprising that they also share traditions and celebrations. Most are still widely observed today, and many are almost unchanged. The majority of festivals celebrate the seasons, including the coming of spring with its promise of fertility and strong plant growth, and the arrival of summer to ripen the fruits and welcome the bountiful harvests from the sea.

New Year

The beginning of the year is an important event in both countries. On New Year's Eve in Romania, children sing songs and play games, and people dance wearing masks of goats, bears and other ancient sun-worship icons. On New Year's Day, children wish everyone a good year to come by touching the adults with a bouquet of coloured paper flowers.

In Bulgaria, New Year's Day is St Basil's Day, or *Survaki*. The New Year period is a time of enthusiastic festivities, involving cultural events, carnivals, music festivals and often a holiday trip to one of the many beautiful beaches. A traditional Bulgarian New Year's dish is banitsa, a flaky cheese pie.

Trifon Zarezan

In February, Bulgarians celebrate the patron saint of wine and vine growers, St Trifon, or *Trifon Zarezan*. The word *zarezan* means 'snub nose', and the story goes that the vine grower Trifon was ordered by the Virgin Mary to cut off the tip of his nose with his own pruning shears as a punishment for mocking her.

The date for *Trifon Zarezan* was set by the religious calendar as 1 February, but since the 1990s the festival has been celebrated on 14 February. As this is the same day as St Valentine's Day, which has only recently been celebrated in Bulgaria, people now celebrate wine and love on the same occasion.

The festivities include rituals performed as the vines are pruned: blessings and prayers for strong vines and an abundant harvest. They also cut three twigs from three different vines, ritually wash the cuts and twine the twigs together. The women bake festive loaves decorated with vine-shaped dough and grapes, and roast chicken stuffed with ground corn, as well as filling flasks of wine to give to the men.

Mărțișor/Martenitsa

On the first day of March, Romanians celebrate the beginning of spring. Females are given a *Mărțișor*: a double-threaded red-and-white string, usually with a small trinket. This is pinned to the lapel, worn for a week, and then tied to a flowering tree to bring good luck and a bountiful crop. In Bulgaria this is known as *Martenitsa* and the token is given to males and females, as well as attached to greetings cards and sent to Bulgarian communities worldwide.

Kukerov Den festival

This Bulgarian festival falls on the first Sunday before Lent. It celebrates the start of the agricultural year, and is characterized by processions led by the *Kukeri*, dancing men with grotesque masks and colourful costumes. Their dances are believed to dispel evil spirits and ensure a productive season.

Easter

Both countries celebrate Easter according to the Eastern Orthodox Church. In Romania, the Friday before

ABOVE Two women in Bulgarian national costume during the Festival of the Roses.

ABOVE An Easter service at St Alexander Nevsky Cathedral in Sofia, Bulgaria.

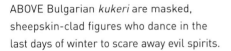
ABOVE Bulgarian *kukeri* are masked, sheepskin-clad figures who dance in the last days of winter to scare away evil spirits.

Easter is called Great Friday or the Friday of Sufferings. Midnight mass is celebrated on Saturday, and the congregation take a bowl of pasca (a traditional Easter cake), eggs and steak to be blessed. Eggs are also painted using thin sticks.

In Bulgaria, churchgoers will fast for six weeks before Easter, during which fast all animal products are avoided. Palm Sunday, or *Vrubnitsa*, marks the start of Holy Week, which leads up to the festival of the Resurrection on Easter Sunday. For the less devout, Easter activities involve the lighting of candles in churches, the decoration of eggs, and the making of Bulgarian breads known as kolache or kozunak. On the Saturday before Easter Sunday, people take red painted eggs and bread to a midnight service.

St George's Day
In Romania, St George's Day is celebrated on 23 April and in Bulgaria on 6 May. This heralds the end of spring and the start of summer. On St George's Eve people decorate their houses with beech twigs and blossoming hawthorn or lilac, and women throw plants and herbs into local wells for good health.

ABOVE Romanian men and boys wearing bear masks dance in central Bucharest as they perform to an ancient winter carol.

In the past, special breads were made but today Bulgarian households prefer to cook a whole lamb in honour of St George, the patron saint of shepherds.

Kazanluk Rose Festival
Bulgaria is one of the major producers of rose oil, made from the Kazanluk rose that has been cultivated for more than 300 years. The production of rose oil is labour-intensive, with 3,000kg/6,500lb of roses required to produce just 1 litre/1¾ pints of rose oil. This harvest was first celebrated in 1903 in Kazanluk. The workers would dress in petals and parade around the village. In later years the festival spread to nearby towns and villages, and was eventually declared a national celebration. People from the whole of the Valley of Roses celebrate in early June each year, when a Rose Queen is elected; there is a ritual harvest in the rose garden and a parade along the streets of Kazanluk.

The Feast of St Nicholas
On 6 December is one of the most important festivals: St Nicholas' Day (in Bulgaria *Nikulden* or in Romania *Nikoline*), the great winter festival that

celebrates the patron saint of the sea, rivers and lakes, fish, mermaids and water demons – and of children. In Romania on the evening of the 5 December, members of the family polish their boots and leave them by the front door. During the night, St Nicholas visits and leaves small presents in each.

Carp is traditionally eaten on St Nicholas' Day. In Bulgaria it is wrapped in dough – called ribnik – and baked with traditional bread. The ribnik and bread are blessed, then small pieces are offered to the neighbours. The rest is eaten by the family for supper.

Christmas
In Bulgaria, Christmas Eve involves a festive family dinner with a minimum of 12 dishes. These dishes never include meat, instead featuring beans, nuts, dried plums, cakes and a pie called banitsa, as well as traditional alcoholic drinks such as rakia.

In Romania, Christmas begins with a strict six-week Advent. On 20 December, Ignat Day, an old medieval custom unique to Romania takes place: the sacrifice of a pig. The meat is then prepared to make all kinds of pork specialities for the Christmas meal, such as toba (a sort of pâté), caltabos (sausages) and piftie (aspic).

A diverse cuisine

The food and cooking of Romania and Bulgaria have many similarities. Meat dishes are a strong feature, and one-pot meals, cabbage rolls, sausages and stews are representative of both cuisines. Each country also has individual characteristics. Bulgaria's rich vegetable crop means that stuffed vegetables and salads are a strong component of the diet, and Romania is noted for its filling soups, its love of mămăligă, made from yellow maize, or polenta, and an exciting variety of local cheeses.

ROMANIAN COOKING: A BLEND OF CULTURES

Romania has an exciting and diverse gastronomy, with influences from Austria, Hungary, Italy, Germany, Turkey and Greece, as well as the Slavic countries.

The three main historical regions, Transylvania, Wallachia and Moldavia, have developed different culinary traditions. Transylvania, in the north-west, was ruled by the Hungarian kingdom for many centuries. Here, garlic soup and the more piquant dishes spiced with paprika are popular, because the favoured variety of sweet red (bell) pepper is widely grown

in Hungary. Wallachia, which was under Ottoman rule for hundreds of years, today boasts variants of Turkish and Greek dishes such as the sweet pastry baklava, ciorba (soups), guvech (stew), sarmale (stuffed cabbage leaves) and musaca (moussaka). In Moldavia, on the border with Ukraine, typical Russian dishes such as borscht and kasha are prepared.

Traditional foods for every day

Romanians have a healthy diet of fresh foods, because it is easy for them to buy inexpensive fruit and vegetables. A typical start to the day will include bread, eggs, telemea cheese,

cucumber, tomatoes and sausage or salami. As in most countries of south-eastern Europe, breakfast will be accompanied by black coffee, but with the rise of American-style coffee chains, white coffee is now becoming more popular. More established breakfast dishes include mămăligă, which is similar to Italian polenta. This dish is a local tradition in the countryside, served combined with feta cheese, sour milk or butter, and with a glass of goat's milk to accompany the meal.

Lunch is the main meal of the day, consisting of three courses. Tradition dictates that families eat lunch together every weekend. The meal will invariably begin with a soup, or ciorba, perhaps of tripe, or with meatballs or vegetables. A hot course

BELOW A butcher arranges sausages during the annual pork festival in Balvanyos, Romania.

BELOW A Romanian woman preparing pastry for a cheese pie in Caraorman, a village in the Danube Delta.

follows of meat or fish and seasonal vegetables. Sometimes, the meat and vegetables will be served in a stew or casserole. For dessert there will be fruit or a pastry.

The Romanian family like to come together at dinner time and the meal may begin with a salad followed by sarmale (minced meat wrapped in cabbage) or guvech (a Turkish-style casserole made with or without meat), or perhaps a veal escalope or kebab accompanied by a selection of root or pickled vegetables. Romanians will often drink wine or țuică, a locally produced plum liqueur, with their meal.

Getting together with friends

Romanians are among the most hospitable of peoples, and the many large speciality dishes in their cuisine are perfectly suited to large gatherings where guests can help themselves.

When visiting, it is customary for guests to bring a gift for their hosts, usually a bottle of liqueur or some food that can be consumed during the evening. Guests will normally be greeted with a glass of liqueur.

There is usually plenty of food and drink to enjoy and many hosts consider it impolite to refuse offers for more food. Dinner will inevitably be interspersed with loud toasts, to the food and to the host, and an exchange of anecdotes or stories. Social events tend to go on well into the night, as guests stay to chat or make merry for many hours.

ABOVE LEFT A food and drink vendor in a street kiosk waiting for customers in Bucharest, Romania.
ABOVE Preparing traditional polenta over an open fire in a herdsman's house in Romania.
BELOW In the summer, street cafés line the Piata Sfatului or Council Square, at the heart of medieval Brașov in Romania.

BULGARIAN COOKING: A MIX OF FRESH INGREDIENTS

The cuisine of Bulgaria has been shaped not only by foreign influences, particularly those of Turkey, Greece and Serbia, but also by the favourable weather. The hot climate produces excellent-quality fresh fruit and vegetables and so salads and vegetable dishes form a significant element of the diet.

Variety is the daily spice of life

Bulgarians have an unusually varied diet; the popularity of ready-made meals has not taken hold in Bulgaria and the pace of life is generally slower than in western Europe, so it allows time for preparing more of the speciality dishes. For breakfast, Bulgarians will most commonly eat some type of cheese, either kashkaval or feta, with lukanka, a unique Bulgarian salami, accompanied by fresh tomatoes and cucumbers. Ayran, or coffee, will most typically be drunk in the morning.

More fresh produce appears on the lunchtime menu, starting with a salad, such as a shopska salata – chunks of

RIGHT A diner serving herself from a dish of Bulgarian sauerkraut stew.

tomato, cucumber, (bell) peppers, onions, and cheese – or a lighter bean salad. To follow, a hot vegetable dish such as roasted vegetables may accompany meatballs or kebabcheta, sausage-like pieces of minced meat.

Dinner is the main meal of the day, and this three-course meal will usually begin with salad, or perhaps a cheese delicacy, such as kashkaval pane, a popular dish of fried yellow cheese. Main courses at dinner can vary from season to season. In winter, when vegetables and fruit are not so readily available, heavier rice or potato dishes are eaten, such as moussaka or chicken with potatoes. In summer, the meal will be simpler and lighter, perhaps grilled (broiled) meat or fish accompanied by fried courgettes (zucchini) or aubergines (eggplants), or with summer stone fruits or grapes. For dessert, baklava is popular, or for a more substantial and traditional dish, a pastry (banitsa) might be prepared with a sweet pumpkin filling.

A warm welcome

The people of Bulgaria (and Romania) are convivial, warm-hearted and always ready to welcome visitors. The Slavic saying khlyap i sol means 'bread and salt' and it demonstrates Bulgarian hospitality: guests are often welcomed with a piece of special bread, which is then dipped in salt and tasted. Guests will also be welcomed with a glass of rakia, a type of brandy, or the aniseed liqueur mastika.

For larger gatherings there will usually be a large buffet available for guests, containing bread, various dips such as kyopolou (aubergine dip) and lyutenitsa (a hot relish made from tomatoes and red peppers) as well as grilled vegetables. A large buffet such as this is sometimes called mezze and can go on for hours, accompanied by many toasts. The drinking of rakia will follow throughout the evening, and is also drunk at every toast – indeed, it is considered improper to toast with the wrong alcohol.

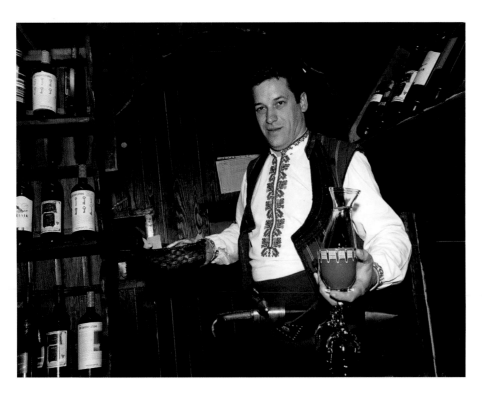

LEFT Traditional food is served in a restaurant in Bansko in the Pirin Mountains.

RIGHT Preparing bread dough in a traditional kitchen in Gabrovo, Bulgaria.

Bulgarians are generous people and will worry if they see that a guest's plate is empty. It is therefore wise to leave a little food on the plate, to avoid having to refuse any offers of food if you are full. At events of particular note, the meal may be followed by traditional Bulgarian folk dancing or music.

Foreign influences

Early tribes such as the Bulgars, the Slavs and the Huns settled in Bulgaria at various points in its history and made their mark on the cuisine, along with the powerful empires that dominated the country, including the Byzantine Empire in the 11th century and the Ottoman Empire in the 13th century. There is also the ever-present influence of neighbouring countries, such as Greece, Turkey, Serbia and Hungary.

Greek cuisine brought to Bulgaria some of the most popular dishes, such as moussaka, which is eaten with chunks of potato rather than aubergine,

as is traditional in Greece. Inevitably, there are a huge number of originally Turkish dishes that have become Bulgarian over hundreds of years of Ottoman rule. Dishes such as sarmi (stuffed cabbage leaves) and baklava have been cooked and prepared for over 500 years and are fully incorporated

into the Bulgarian heritage. There is also a central-Asian influence in Bulgarian cuisine: yogurt was most likely to have been introduced to Bulgaria by one if its earliest founding tribes, the Volga Bulgars.

National and regional specialities

Even after 500 years of Ottoman rule and a difficult time under communism when food was scarce, Bulgarian cuisine still retains an amazing number of national specialities. Lyutenitsa is a Bulgarian relish made of tomatoes with (bell) peppers, onion, garlic and chilli that is eaten with salads, and also goes well with meat. Kyopolou is a national relish or vegetable caviar, which originated around the Black Sea region of Varna. Consisting of cooked aubergine combined with garlic, it has a distinctive smoky flavour. The rustic salad shopska salata was developed by the shopi people who live around Sofia. Banitsa is a traditional Bulgarian pastry made with cheese, traditionally eaten during Christmas celebrations, but now also eaten at other times.

ABOVE This tomato bake is typical of the Thracian region in southern Bulgaria.

ABOVE Suh tarator is a yogurt salad made from strained thick yogurt and cucumber.

ABOVE Baklava is a classic dessert in Bulgaria, an inheritance from the Ottomans.

Typical ingredients

Romania and Bulgaria stretch from the centre to the south-east of Europe. The contrasting topography within both countries means that the produce is varied, ranging from fruit grown in the foothills of the Carpathians to rice and lentils cultivated in southern Bulgaria. The Danube, a central feature of each country, provides many varieties of fish and also irrigates the surrounding plains. Here is an overview of ingredients that form the backbone of the traditional dishes.

Southern summer crops and northern root crops

Whereas Romanian dishes feature a significant number of root vegetables, the cuisine in Bulgaria tends to use lighter vegetables such as (bell) peppers, aubergines (eggplants) and courgettes (zucchini). Such vegetables often come together in stews, are fried on their own as accompaniments to main meals or feature in rustic salads. All these vegetables may also be hollowed and stuffed with meat or cheese to create delicious side dishes or main meals.

A particular favourite for fresh produce eaten raw is shopska salata, a dressed salad of tomato, cucumber, pepper and feta cheese. It is often eaten as a substantial appetizer or side dish to meat dishes. In the summer, the Bulgarian countryside is weighed down with ripe red peppers, lush blood-red tomatoes and black aubergines, and these are also grown in private gardens and allotments. These vegetables are so prolific that Bulgaria has been described as 'one big salad bowl'.

In Romania, in contrast, root and cruciferous vegetables are more widely eaten, including the strongly flavoured celeriac, cabbage – used in the famous sauerkraut – and onion.

Meat and poultry

In Romania, meat is frequently served grilled (broiled) and is accompanied by a selection of vegetables, the latter often pickled. The most popular meat is pork, which might be grilled, added to stews or minced (ground) to be used as a stuffing. Paprika and (bell) peppers are often partnered with meat to produce spicy dishes. In the northern regions of Romania, beef dishes have Russian and Ukrainian influences, whereas in the region around the Hungarian border dishes using sausages are typical of the influence of Austria and Germany.

Bulgarian meat dishes share many similarities with Romanian ones, but most popular are grilled meats and kebabs. Pork kebabs and meatballs, called kebapche and kyufte, are served with crisp salads made with peppers, tomatoes and cucumber. Minced meat is also commonly used in stuffed peppers and vine leaves, as well as in

ABOVE Celeriac is a widely grown vegetable in Romania, where root vegetables form an integral part of the diet.

ABOVE Aubergines grow well in Bulgaria, where the climate is warm and, in the south distinctly Mediterranean.

ABOVE Pork cuts, such as the pork belly shown here, are commonplace in the everyday cuisine of both countries.

ABOVE Whitebait is fished along the Black Sea coastline and its delicate flavour makes it a popular choice for fried dishes.

ABOVE Cherries form part of the plentiful fruit harvest within Bulgaria and Romania and are a frequent ingredient in desserts.

ABOVE Abundantly grown in Bulgaria, walnuts appear in many of the national dishes, both sweet and savoury.

moussaka. Lamb and rabbit are cooked in Bulgarian dishes with rice or vegetables, such as tomatoes and okra.

Both countries enjoy casseroling meat – the most famous being ghiveci or guvech, a Turkish-style casserole. Chicken is also casseroled or made into schnitzels stuffed with wild mushrooms or cooked on a bed of vegetables and served with a rich sauce.

Fish
Although meat is more popular in both countries, traditional fish dishes exist in the areas around the two main sources of fish: the Danube and the Black Sea. The Danube river acts as the main boundary between Bulgaria and Romania and provides an abundant source of fresh fish for both countries. There are over 60 types of fish in the waters, such as pike, carp, sterlet, sturgeon, sheat fish, crayfish and perch. The sterlet and sturgeon are especially prized for their yield of valuable caviar.

Many different types of fish, including mackerel, mullet, turbot, blue fish, catfish and types of small fish for whitebait, live in the waters of

the Black Sea coastline, and are often prepared in simple, fresh dishes. In both countries, tasty snacks or appetizers of fried fish are much enjoyed. Main-course fish dishes will typically be marinated in a sauce, fried or grilled simply over wood embers and accompanied by salad or vegetables. Fish soups are also prepared, particularly in the Black Sea regions, although soups from the north, such as the Russian-Ukrainian fish soup called uha, tend to be heavier than in the south, where the climate suits broth-type soups better.

Fruit and nuts
In almost every season, there are delicious fresh fruits or nuts available in Bulgaria and Romania, and when fruits are bountiful they are dried to make snacks or accompaniments for meat during the winter months. Almost every household in the countryside has its own vineyard or trees weighed down with plums, apples, peaches and other fruits. The Bulgarian climate is particularly well suited to the cultivation of fruit-bearing trees. Nuts are widely grown

in the hottest regions, and are used in both sweet and savoury dishes. Huge walnut trees are to be found all over southern Bulgaria and the nut is used in yogurts and soups, as well as sweet desserts such as baklava and a torte called garash.

Fruit makes up a significant part of the Bulgarian diet. Huge, sweet honeydew melons and watermelons can be bought extremely cheaply and are eaten as a refreshing snack in the sweltering summers. The plums are dried and eaten as snacks or cooked with chicken.

Fruit growing is widespread in the north of Romania, especially in the foothills of the Carpathians, where cherries, grapes and apples predominate. Cherries are especially abundant in the countryside and mountainous regions, and the fruit is typically used in cherry strudels, an example of the influence of the Austro-Hungarian Empire. Apples and raisins are also widely used in Romanian strudels and pancakes. Grapes are grown all over both countries – for eating fresh as well as for wine making.

ABOVE Yogurt is an important dairy product in the Balkans, eaten on its own and as a component of other dishes.

ABOVE Kashkaval is a hard, yellow sheep's milk cheese (left) and telemea has a soft, creamy texture and a tangy flavour.

ABOVE Polenta is a ground cornmeal; in Russia and Eastern Europe it is traditionally made from buckwheat groats.

Dairy produce

Cheese and yogurt dishes are some of the most popular among Romanians and Bulgarians, eaten either on their own or as accompaniments and marinades. Throughout the Balkans, a yellow cheese called kashkaval has been produced for centuries. In both countries it is eaten in several forms, including fried in large pieces and served with a main course. The other main cheese, feta, typically added to salads, is crumblier than kashkaval and has a stronger taste. In Romania, the equivalent cheese to feta is called telemea, and, with sour milk, it often accompanies the traditional Romanian dish of mămăligă (a type of polenta). The cheeses are traditionally produced around the Danube plains, where cows, sheep and water buffalo graze.

Yogurt dishes appear all over the Balkans, but particularly in Bulgaria, where yogurt is prepared in various forms. Thick sheep's yogurt has been produced for many centuries, going so far back that many Bulgarians have tried to assert that the Greek (US strained plain) yogurt eaten in the West is in fact Bulgarian.

A variety of cold appetizers and soups with yogurt exist in Bulgaria today, including a cold salad called milk salad, or mlechna salata, which is made from thick yogurt and cucumber. Yogurt is also taken as a drink, called ayran, mainly in Bulgaria, Turkey and some other parts of central Asia and the Middle East. Yet another yogurt dish is katuk, made of thickened ewe's milk, which is mixed with Bulgarian feta cheese and sometimes garlic.

Cereals, grains and beans

Cereals have traditionally been the staple foods in Romania, where one of the national dishes is mămăligă, a polenta-like dish made from cornmeal. Although traditionally a peasant food, today it is rather trendy in haute cuisine restaurants. When left to set, it is much thicker than its Italian equivalent of polenta and is sometimes used as a bread substitute. Today it is mostly eaten with meat or cheese and is a healthy alternative to most carbohydrates because it is high in fibre and cholesterol-free. Its Bulgarian equivalent is known as kachamak.

The Thracian valley was the home of numerous rice plantations during the early 18th century, and much of this rice was then shipped to Turkey. Turkish rice recipes have a firm place in the cuisines of both Romania and Bulgaria, including steamed rice pilaffs and a rice pudding called sutliash. Rice has always been a preferred staple in Bulgaria, as opposed to potatoes.

The most popular variety of rice in both Romania and Bulgaria is short grain, which is used in main meals, soups and desserts.

Beans are widely available, and all are locally grown, including many types that are unfamiliar outside Romania and Bulgaria. White-seeded varieties are the most common, such as dobruzanski, astor and trudovetz. Another example is the large smilyan bean that is available in white, black and brown, grown in the Rhodope mountains close to the border with Greece. Beans are often used in soups and stews, such as the Bulgarian national dish, fasul chorba, which is a flavoursome soup made with beans, tomato and herbs.

Bread and pastries

An essential staple in both countries, bread is routinely served to accompany every meal, whether soups, stew, salads or grills. A round, white bread called pogacha is often served hot, filled with a creamy feta cheese and decorated with a sprinkle of local summer herbs. Sandwiches are not widely eaten.

In Bulgaria, banitsa is one of the most popular national dishes. Made from layers of filo pastry, whisked eggs and feta cheese, it can be eaten at any meal but most often at breakfast. At Christmas and other holidays small messages and charms will be put inside the banitsa or on the top. Another popular bread recipe in Bulgaria is the Bird of Paradise Bread, a yeast bread decorated with cheese, ham, peppers and olives.

In Romania, the famous strudel is made with filo pastry wrapped around a filling of poppy seeds, currants, apples or cherries. Another favourite is panetone, or sweet yeasted bread, filled with raisins, walnuts or chocolate. Baklava, a rich and sweet pastry, is a traditional dessert in both countries, an inheritance from the Ottoman Empire.

Herbs, spices and flavourings

In Bulgaria, dill is used to flavour yogurt salads and soups, and it is added to grilled (broiled) vegetables such as courgettes (zucchini). Rose flavourings are popular, because of the famous flowers from Bulgaria's Valley of Roses. Rice pudding is often decorated with the delicately scented rose petals, and rose syrup can be added to baklava.

Traditionally, Romanian cuisine is slightly more piquant than Bulgarian because it uses paprika, an influence from its neighbour, Hungary, where the variety of pepper used for the spice is grown in abundance. It will be found in soups and casseroles as a substitute for black pepper.

A typical herb used in Romanian cooking is lovage or leustean, which people often grow at home. Used mostly in sour soups, lovage has a long history in Romania and was probably introduced by the Roman colonists who settled there after the demise of the Roman Empire.

Thyme, tarragon, parsley and fennel are all also used throughout Bulgaria and Romania to heighten the flavour of the local dishes.

Drinks

Both Romanians and Bulgarians are great lovers of fruit liqueurs, whose ingredients range from rose to aniseed to plum. The Romanians' favourite liqueurs are ţuică, made from plums, which is customarily drunk as a shot alongside a salad or before a meal, and pălincă, which has a 40 per cent pure alcohol content. Both of these are often brewed at home. The equivalent spirit in Bulgaria is called rakia, a fruit brandy that is popular throughout the Balkans, usually made from plums or grapes. Mastica is another well-liked spirit here, an aniseed liqueur formed from the base of rakia.

Both domestic and commercial vineyards are found throughout Bulgaria and Romania, and both countries export a huge amount of wine. Indeed, Romania is the ninth largest exporter of wine in the world.

A favourite non-alcoholic drink in Bulgaria is ayran, a yogurt drink mixed with water and a sprinkling of salt, which is served chilled with meals and makes a refreshing beverage in the summer months.

ABOVE Mămăligă is made from yellow maize. A traditional Romanian dish, it can also be used to make mămăligă bread.

ABOVE Rose water is used to flavour food, and the Valley of the Roses in Kazanluk, Bulgaria, is one of the main producers.

ABOVE Romanian pălincă is a twice-distilled strong plum brandy. The other popular liqueur, ţuică, is less fiery.

APPETIZERS & SIDE DISHES

Many of the dishes in this chapter are vegetable based, made with seasonally available produce such as courgettes, tomatoes and spinach. These vegetable dishes can be stuffed, baked or fried. They are served as accompaniments to a main meal, or as appetizers with cold cuts of meat, sausages, tasty dips, local cheeses and a cold glass of beer. In fact, a favourite Romanian appetizer would be a simple serving of pungent local cheese alongside ţuică (plum brandy) and black olives.

Mezze and mastika

The first stage of a meal in Romania and Bulgaria is rarely a swift affair, often lasting up to an hour long. When appetizers are served, an array of tasty options is offered. A selection of cold dishes will be provided, often accompanied with seasonal salads – especially in Bulgaria (see next chapter) – and small bites of hot home-made sausages, including sujuk in Bulgaria and mititei in Romania. Appetizers in Romania are typically served on a large platter, and include sliced salami, fried sausages, chopped vegetables, boiled eggs and mayonnaise.

In the style of their Mediterranean neighbours, Turkey and Greece, fresh vegetables such as aubergine and courgette feature prominently in both countries, along with olive oil, garlic, goat's cheese, ham and anchovies. While the Mediterranean influence is strong, many dishes also have an Eastern twist, evident in the use of spices. Another Eastern European preference is dishes where food is hidden within other food, such as stuffed peppers and stuffed eggs; those here include vine leaves and stuffed tomatoes.

The people of both countries often accompany the first stage of a meal with alcohol, typically mastika (an anise drink) or rakia (grape brandy) in Bulgaria, or țuică (plum brandy) and the breathtakingly strong pălincă (made from fermented plums, peaches and apricots) in Romania.

Serves 4
225g/8oz nettles
50g/2oz/¼ cup butter
1 onion, finely chopped
2 large garlic cloves, finely chopped
pinch of cayenne pepper
1 litre/1¾ pints/4 cups hot
    vegetable stock
75ml/5 tbsp cooked pudding rice
    (35ml/2½ tbsp raw weight)
4 eggs
salt and ground black pepper

Bulgarian Nettle Kasha with Poached Egg

The eating of kasha goes back many centuries and the term usually refers to a dish prepared using buckwheat groats. In this recipe of nettle tops cooked in a stock with rice, however, the Slavic term kasha refers to a texture rather than a particular ingredient.

1 Wash the nettles and discard the tough parts.

2 Melt the butter in a large pan and cook the onion and garlic over medium heat for 5 minutes, or until softened but not browned. Season with salt, black pepper and cayenne pepper.

3 Add the nettles and sauté briefly. Add the stock and cooked rice, and simmer for 10 minutes.

4 Liquidize (blend) until smooth, then return to the pan and bring to the boil, stirring constantly. Crack each of the eggs and drop them one at a time into the hot liquid to poach, stirring very gently.

5 Serve while hot, with an egg for each portion, sprinkled with a little cayenne pepper.

COOK'S TIPS
• Pick the very top, young nettle leaves; they are best at the beginning of the season.
• Nettles are also good in salads, and can be cooked like spinach.

PER SERVING: Energy 229kcal/949kJ; Protein 9.1g; Carbohydrate 11.8g, of which sugars 3.7g; Fat 16.4g, of which saturates 8.4g; Cholesterol 219mg; Calcium 140mg; Fibre 1.9g; Sodium 244mg.

Serves 4
8 medium ripe tomatoes
40g/1½oz/3 tbsp butter
1 onion, chopped
200g/7oz/1 cup white long grain rice
80g/3¼oz/¾ cup pine nuts
115g/4oz feta cheese, crumbled
30ml/2 tbsp chopped fresh parsley
salt and ground black pepper

Tomatoes with Feta and Pine Nut Stuffing

When tomatoes are at their most refreshing and sweet, try stuffing them with a delicious mixture of feta cheese, rice and pine nuts. Feta is very popular in Bulgaria, where it is called sirene, and in Romania, where it is called telemea.

1 Preheat the oven to 180°C/350°F/ Gas 4. Cut a slice from the top of each tomato and set aside (to be used as lids). Remove the seeds and pulp from the tomatoes using a teaspoon. Reserve the pulp and seeds.

2 Arrange the hollowed-out tomatoes in a shallow baking dish.

3 Melt the butter in a medium pan, cook the onion until soft over medium heat, then add the tomato pulp and seeds. Meanwhile, cook the rice in boiling water for about 12 minutes, or until semi-cooked. Drain and add to the onion and tomato, with the pine nuts, cheese and parsley.

4 Season well with salt and pepper, and stir well. Fill the tomatoes with the mixture, and replace the lid on each. Put in the hot oven and bake for about 30 minutes. Serve hot as an appetizer or cold as a snack.

COOK'S TIP
This is a good dish to prepare earlier in the day and then it can be baked directly before serving.

PER SERVING: Energy 511kcal/2123kJ; Protein 12.9g; Carbohydrate 50.5g, of which sugars 9.4g; Fat 28.6g, of which saturates 10.4g; Cholesterol 43mg; Calcium 142mg; Fibre 2.8g; Sodium 507mg.

Filo and Feta Cheese Pie

Banitsa is the name given to this Bulgarian cheese pie, which is a popular dish usually made with creamy Bulgarian feta cheese mixed with vegetables, spinach, courgettes, chard leaves or sorrel. Traditionally, this pie is made in a distinctive spiral shape. You can also make small individual portions in the same coil shapes.

Serves 8
400g/14oz filo pastry, thawed if frozen
65g/2½oz/5 tbsp butter, melted

For the filling
10ml/2 tsp olive oil
8 spring onions (scallions), diced
800g/1¾lb spinach, stalks removed
200g/7oz feta cheese, crumbled
115g/4oz/1 cup grated mild
   Cheddar cheese
2 eggs, beaten
1 bunch mint, finely chopped
salt and ground black pepper

COOK'S TIPS
• The less cooked the spinach, the crunchier it is, making the best consistency for this pie.
• Another vegetable that can easily be combined with the other ingredients in this dish is cooked pumpkin.

1 Preheat the oven to 180°C/350°F/Gas 4. Grease a large, round baking dish, about 20–23cm/8–9in in diameter.

2 To make the filling, heat the olive oil in a large, deep pan, add the onions and spinach, and cook for 1–2 minutes, or until the spinach leaves have wilted. Season to taste with salt and pepper.

3 Remove the onions and spinach with a slotted spoon and transfer to a large bowl. Add the feta cheese, Cheddar cheese, eggs and mint. Mix well.

4 To arrange the banitsa, lay a filo sheet on a work surface. (Cover the remaining filo pastry with a damp dish towel to prevent it from drying out.) Brush the filo sheet with melted butter, then top with another filo sheet.

5 Spoon about 30ml/2 tbsp of filling along the long edge of the filo sheet, leaving 2cm/¾in on each side. Fold in the ends and roll the pastry up over the filling. Repeat with the remaining filo sheets and filling.

6 To form the banitsa, shape the rolls into a large spiral shape by firmly coiling them around each other in the baking dish. Brush the tops generously with melted butter.

7 Bake for 30–35 minutes, or until the top is golden. Serve as an appetizer, snack or side dish, hot, warm or cold.

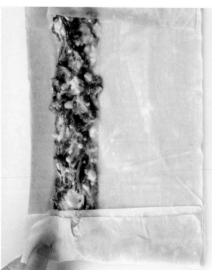
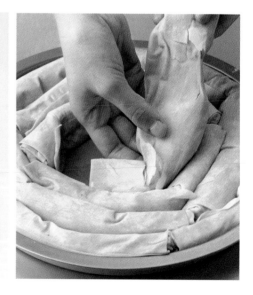

PER SERVING: Energy 394kcal/1645kJ; Protein 17g; Carbohydrate 33.4g, of which sugars 2.8g; Fat 22g, of which saturates 12g; Cholesterol 132mg; Calcium 440mg; Fibre 3.5g; Sodium 697mg.

Thracian Tomato Bake

This dish, trakiiski guvech, is typical of the Thracian region in southern Bulgaria. It is the perfect light supper dish, served with crusty bread to soak those delicious juices, and a green salad. A little Parmesan is added to the tomatoes, which is not traditional but adds richness.

1 Preheat the oven to 180°C/350°F/ Gas 4. Oil a 40 x 50cm/16 x 20in baking tray or similar size dish, and arrange half the sliced tomatoes over the base, overlapping them slightly.

2 Sprinkle with some of the parsley, salt and pepper, and repeat with another layer of tomatoes, parsley and seasoning.

3 Put the breadcrumbs, Parmesan, paprika and chilli in a bowl and mix well together. Sprinkle over the top of the layered tomatoes. Bake for 45 minutes, or until golden brown. Serve hot or cold.

COOK'S TIP
The perfect accompaniment to this dish is a cold cucumber, mint and yogurt salad.

Serves 4–6
45ml/3 tbsp olive oil
1kg/2¼lb ripe plum tomatoes, sliced
small bunch of parsley, leaves
    finely chopped
45ml/3 tbsp fresh breadcrumbs
30ml/2 tbsp freshly grated
    Parmesan cheese
5ml/1 tsp ground paprika
2.5ml/½ tsp mild chilli powder
salt and ground black pepper

PER SERVING: Energy 130kcal/546kJ; Protein 4.2g; Carbohydrate 11.4g, of which sugars 5.4g; Fat 7.9g, of which saturates 2g; Cholesterol 5mg; Calcium 84mg; Fibre 1.8g; Sodium 127mg.

Serves 6

90–120ml/6–8 tbsp olive oil
6 pale-green courgettes (zucchini)
60–75ml/4–5 tbsp plain (all-purpose) flour

For the sauce

200ml/7fl oz/scant 1 cup thick natural
  (plain) yogurt
3 garlic cloves, crushed
5 mint sprigs, leaves finely chopped
30ml/2 tbsp olive oil
30ml/2 tbsp chopped walnuts
salt and ground black pepper

VARIATION

This dish can be varied by adding fried
aubergine (eggplant) slices.

Pan-fried Courgettes with Yogurt and Garlic Sauce

This simple recipe with lightly fried crispy courgettes, served with yogurt and garlic sauce, is delicious served as a side dish on a long, warm summer's evening. Preferably use pale courgettes at the peak of their season, although darker ones will also work well.

1 Slice the courgettes into 5mm/¼in slices. Put in a bowl and add the flour, mixing together gently until all the courgette slices are coated. Remove and arrange on a platter, discard the excess flour.

2 Heat 60ml/4 tbsp oil in a large frying pan and add the courgettes, a few at a time, frying over medium heat for 2–3 minutes on each side,

or until just golden brown. Remove with a slotted spoon and drain on kitchen paper. Keep warm while you cook the remaining courgette slices, adding more oil if required.

3 To make the sauce, put the yogurt, garlic, mint and olive oil in a bowl and mix well. Season to taste, and then add the walnuts. Serve the courgettes with the yogurt and garlic sauce.

PER SERVING: Energy 250kcal/1033kJ; Protein 5g; Carbohydrate 6.9g, of which sugars 4.9g; Fat 22.7g, of which saturates 3g; Cholesterol 0mg; Calcium 117mg; Fibre 1.7g; Sodium 32mg.

**Serves 6 as a side dish or appetizer;
4 as a main course**
675g/1½lb spinach
2 eggs, beaten
60ml/4 tbsp dried breadcrumbs
50g/2oz kashkaval, or Gruyère
   cheese, grated
1 small bunch parsley, finely chopped
60ml/4 tbsp olive oil
salt and ground black pepper
mayonnaise, to serve

Spinach Fritters

These fritters are a vegetarian version of a Turkish meatball called köfte. They are much loved in Romania (where they are called chiftele) and Bulgaria (where they are called kyufte), and often contain potatoes, although here breadcrumbs are used for a lighter texture. Spinach, abundant in the spring and summer, is combined with kashkaval cheese.

1 Put the spinach in a pan with just the water that is clinging to its leaves after it has been washed, and cook until wilted. Season to taste. Drain and squeeze dry as much as you can. Chop roughly and put into a bowl.

2 Add the beaten eggs, breadcrumbs, cheese and parsley to the spinach and mix well to combine. Season to taste.

3 Divide the mixture into 10–12 small mounds, roll each one into a ball and lightly flatten into a patty.

4 Heat the oil in a frying pan, and when just hot, add two spinach fritters to cook for 3–4 minutes on each side, or until lightly brown. Keep warm while you cook the remaining fritters. Serve immediately, with a dollop of mayonnaise.

VARIATION
Other greens that can be used in this recipe include frozen spinach, watercress, chard leaves or roughly chopped mixed herbs.

PER SERVING: Energy 198kcal/824kJ; Protein 9.2g; Carbohydrate 9.8g, of which sugars 2.2g; Fat 13.7g, of which saturates 3.8g; Cholesterol 73mg; Calcium 304mg; Fibre 3g; Sodium 332mg.

Makes 12

3 large (US extra large) eggs
25g/1oz/2 tbsp butter, melted
250ml/8fl oz/1 cup milk
200ml/7fl oz/scant 1 cup sparkling water
185g/6½oz/1⅔ cups plain
   (all-purpose) flour
45–60ml/3–4 tbsp vegetable oil
60–90ml/4–6 tbsp clarified butter
75–90ml/5–6 tbsp fried, crispy
   breadcrumbs

For the filling

400g/14oz chard leaves, chopped
250g/9oz feta cheese, crumbled
50g/2oz/½ cup grated kashkaval or
   Gruyère cheese
1 garlic clove, crushed
pinch of freshly grated nutmeg
salt and ground black pepper

Feta and Chard Pancakes

This recipe, clatite cu brînză şi lobodă, is from the Romanian region of Moldova. The pancakes are not dissimilar to the thin French-style crêpes. Feta cheese is a staple ingredient in Bulgarian and Romanian cookery.

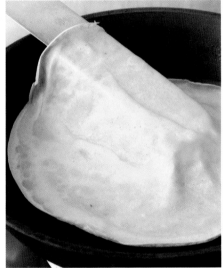

1 To make the filling, half-fill a pan with water, bring to the boil, add the chard leaves and simmer for 3–4 minutes to blanch them. Drain and set aside.

2 Put the feta cheese and kashkaval or Gruyère cheese in a large bowl, then add the garlic and nutmeg. Season with just a little salt and pepper.

3 Squeeze the blanched chard and add to the cheese. Combine well.

4 To make the pancake batter, put the eggs in a food processor with the butter, milk and water, and process to combine. Gradually add the flour and continue to process until smooth.

5 Add a little oil to a medium frying pan and heat over medium heat.

6 Spoon in 45–60ml/3–4 tbsp of the batter and tilt around to spread evenly over the base of the frying pan. Cook for about a minute, until lightly browned, then turn over to cook on the other side. Repeat with the remaining batter and set aside. Keep warm while you make the remaining pancakes.

7 When you are ready, put a generous tablespoon of the filling in the middle of each pancake and spread evenly, then fold the pancake in half, and then in half again.

8 Brush a frying pan with the clarified butter and heat over medium heat, then add the folded pancakes and sauté, for 2 minutes on each side, or until golden and crisp, brushing with butter. Serve hot with a sprinkle of the breadcrumbs.

PER SERVING: Energy 261kcal/1089kJ; Protein 10g; Carbohydrate 18.7g, of which sugars 2.3g; Fat 16.7g, of which saturates 8.7g; Cholesterol 93mg; Calcium 227mg; Fibre 1.3g; Sodium 510mg.

Stuffed Vine Leaves with Cinnamon Yogurt

Bulgaria and Romania are renowned wine-producing regions, and many of their recipes use vine leaves. This Bulgarian recipe, surmis teleshko, uses bulgur wheat instead of rice, and a touch of cinnamon. Romanian dishes that feature stuffed vine leaves, sarmale în foi de vită, are usually combined with rice.

Makes 35–40; serves 8–10

65g/2½oz/generous ½ cup pine nuts
1.5ml/¼ tsp cumin seeds
75g/3oz/½ cup coarse bulgur wheat
40 vine leaves (fresh or in brine), allow
  for some breakage
45ml/3 tbsp extra virgin olive oil
3 shallots, very finely chopped
350g/12oz/1½ cups minced (ground) veal
  or pork
25g/1oz/2 tbsp currants
6 ripe apricots, finely chopped
30ml/2 tbsp chopped fresh dill
30ml/2 tbsp chopped fresh mint
salt and ground black pepper
200g/7oz/scant 1 cup thick natural
  (plain) yogurt, to serve
2.5ml/½ tsp ground cinnamon, to garnish

COOK'S TIPS
• Soaking the bulgur grains helps to make the cooking faster.
• Use fresh vine leaves if you can get them, although preserved leaves will also work well.

1 Put the pine nuts in a dry pan and toast over medium-high heat, tossing regularly, for 1–2 minutes, or until golden brown. Chop and set side. Toast the cumin seeds quickly in a dry pan, then remove from the pan and crush using a mortar and pestle. Set aside. Put the bulgur wheat in a large bowl, add hot water and allow to soak for 30 minutes.

2 If you are using freshly picked vine leaves, put the leaves in a bowl and cover with hot water. Stand for 5 minutes, then drain. If you are using leaves in brine, put them into a bowl and cover with cold water to soak for 15 minutes, then drain.

3 Put the oil in a heavy pan and add the shallots. Sauté gently for 3 minutes, stirring constantly. Add the minced veal or pork and cook until browned, then add the pine nuts, currants, apricots, dill, mint and crushed cumin seeds. Mix well to combine all the ingredients.

4 Drain the bulgur wheat and add to the meat mixture. Mix together and add 60ml/4 tbsp water. Cook for 5 minutes, stirring constantly.

5 Lay a vine leaf face up on a work surface in front of you and put a teaspoonful of the filling on to the centre of the leaf, tuck in the sides and then roll away from you to form a small sausage shape. Repeat with the remaining leaves; allow for the fact that some of them will break.

6 Put the broken vine leaves over the base of a medium pan and then arrange the stuffed vine leaves on top, placing them tightly up against one another. Add enough water to cover and put a plate on top to weigh down the leaves, so that they will stay as you have arranged them. Cover the pan and simmer for 30 minutes.

PER SERVING: Energy 152kcal/635kJ; Protein 9.7g; Carbohydrate 10.5g, of which sugars 6.5g; Fat 8.2g, of which saturates 1.7g; Cholesterol 23mg; Calcium 60mg; Fibre 1.1g; Sodium 42mg.

VEGETABLE DISHES & SALADS

Mediterranean-style vegetables and sustaining root crops are common to both Romania and Bulgaria, and crispy, colourful salads are a speciality of the latter, where they often introduce a meal. Both countries have a strong rural tradition, with produce that's organic because chemicals and fertilizers are rarely used – so vegetables are fresh and wholesome. Crunchy raw crudités are enjoyed with dips and spreads, and warm dishes include caviars, fritters and stuffed vegetables.

Crisp and fresh Mediterranean delights

During the summer months, Bulgaria and Romania harvest an amazing range of fruit and vegetables. The most popular salads are made from tender, crisp lettuce with fresh pink radishes, milky spring onions and plenty of cucumbers and tomatoes. Bulgaria is known as the 'salad bowl' of the Balkans – salads are common fare there, especially during the hot summers, often served with yogurt-based dressings. They are not so widely prepared in Romania, where the preference is for simple slices of seasonal raw vegetables such as tomatoes, cucumbers, radishes and spring onions served as a side dish, or combined with olives and grilled offcuts of meat as an appetizer.

Vegetable staples of the Romanian diet are based on cabbage and root vegetables such as potatoes, onions and carrots, whereas Bulgaria has more green vegetables including okra, green beans, cucumbers, courgettes, spinach and sorrel. During the summer months, cabbage may be prepared and stored as sauerkraut, and peppers and cucumbers and other vegetables such as gherkins and cabbage will be made into spicy pickles for use throughout the year. The aubergine is grown widely in Bulgaria, and is an established ingredient in the dishes of both countries, such as in the kyopolu and the Crisp Aubergine, Feta and Caramelized Shallot Salad. Red peppers are another essential vegetable, used both in salads and in warm dishes.

Makes 400g/14oz
500g/1¼lb long red (bell) peppers
3 red chillies
3 plum tomatoes
2.5ml/½ tsp salt
2 garlic cloves, crushed
60ml/4 tbsp sunflower oil

Red Pepper Caviar

Bulgarians are extremely fond of what they call vegetable caviars, and this particular version is called lyutenitsa in Bulgarian, or ardei roşii umpluti cu caviar in Romania. These days it is commercially available, but nothing beats a home-made version. The best peppers to use are the long red peppers characteristic of Bulgaria. They have soft flesh and a sweet flavour.

1 If cooking with gas, spear the peppers with a long-handled fork or clamp them with tongs and hold directly above the naked flame of the gas ring, turning until the whole pepper is charred and soft. If using an electric stove, put the whole pepper on top of your hot plate and cook, turning, as for gas. This can also be done on a barbecue or under a grill (broiler).

2 Grill the chillies and the tomatoes until blackened on all sides. You are just chargrilling the outside flesh; you don't want to burn the insides.

3 Peel and seed the peppers and the chillies, then put into a food processor or blender and whiz to make a coarse purée. Chop the tomatoes by hand.

4 Put the puréed peppers and chillies, tomatoes, salt and garlic into a large pan over medium heat. Stir to combine and gradually add the oil. Simmer for 10–15 minutes, or until the mixture has thickened.

5 Cool and store in the refrigerator; it will keep for up to a week.

PER SERVING: Energy 600kcal/2484kJ; Protein 7.9g; Carbohydrate 38.6g, of which sugars 37.1g; Fat 46.9g, of which saturates 6g; Cholesterol 0mg; Calcium 69mg; Fibre 10g; Sodium 42mg.

Serves 4

4 long red (bell) peppers
30ml/2 tbsp plain (all-purpose) flour
1 egg, beaten
60–75ml/4–5 tbsp fresh breadcrumbs
60–90ml/4–6 tbsp olive oil

For the filling

115g/4oz feta cheese, crumbled
1 egg
30ml/2 tbsp finely chopped fresh parsley
30ml/2 tbsp finely chopped fresh dill
30ml/2 tbsp finely chopped fresh thyme
salt and ground black pepper

Red Pepper Bürek

This traditional vegetarian dish from Bulgaria uses peppers stuffed with creamy feta cheese and fresh herbs. The best results are achieved when using long red peppers. Serve with a crisp green salad.

1 If cooking with gas, spear the peppers with a long-handled fork and hold directly above the naked flame of the gas ring, turning until the whole pepper is charred and soft. If using an electric stove, put the whole pepper on top of your hot plate and cook, turning, as for gas. This can be done on a barbecue or under a grill (broiler).

2 Put the peppers into a bowl, cover with a dish towel and leave to steam for 10 minutes before peeling the blackened skins, opening them out and cutting out the cores and seeds.

3 To make the filling, put the feta cheese, egg and herbs in a bowl and mix well to combine. Season to taste.

4 Divide the filling equally among the peppers and roll them. Dip each roll in flour, then dip in the egg. Finally, roll the peppers in the breadcrumbs to coat them.

5 Put the oil into a large frying pan and heat over medium heat. Add the peppers and cook for 8–10 minutes, turning every so often to cook evenly on all sides. Serve immediately.

PER SERVING: Energy 320kcal/1331kJ; Protein 10.3g; Carbohydrate 27.6g, of which sugars 11.8g; Fat 19.4g, of which saturates 6.1g; Cholesterol 68mg; Calcium 182mg; Fibre 4.1g; Sodium 501mg.

Serves 4
30ml/2 tbsp olive oil
600g/1lb 5oz sauerkraut, finely chopped
5ml/1 tsp sweet paprika
2 bayleaves
200ml/7fl oz/scant 1 cup chicken stock
salt and ground black pepper

Braised Sauerkraut with Sweet Paprika

When cabbages are in season many people in Bulgaria and Romania make their own sauerkraut, a delicious way to preserve cabbage. Nowadays, it is available in most supermarkets, so if you can't get your hands on a home-made version, use a store-bought variety instead. This recipe is a simple dish, often served as main course.

1 Heat the oil in a large pan; when hot, stir in the sauerkraut. Season with pepper and just a little salt. Add the paprika and mix in well.

2 Add the bayleaves and the chicken stock to the pan, bring to the boil and simmer for 20 minutes. Meanwhile, preheat the oven to 180°C/350°F/Gas 4.

3 Transfer the cabbage with the cooking juices to a baking tray and put in the oven to finish cooking for a further 20 minutes. Serve hot, with crusty bread.

COOK'S TIPS
Sauerkraut has a number of uses:
• It can be added to chicken and pork stews or turkey dishes.
• It often features in chilled salads, where it can be seasoned with oil and paprika.
• It is used to stuff cabbage rolls.
• The salty brine of sauerkraut is commonly used in Bulgaria as a soup base, or as a good cure for a hangover.

PER SERVING: Energy 67kcal/273kJ; Protein 1.8g; Carbohydrate 2.1g, of which sugars 1.7g; Fat 5.7g, of which saturates 0.8g; Cholesterol 0mg; Calcium 77mg; Fibre 3.3g; Sodium 886mg.

Serves 4
1 large onion, grated
30ml/2 tbsp olive oil
450g/1lb courgettes (zucchini), grated
1 large (US extra large) egg
45ml/3 tbsp plain (all-purpose) flour
1 small bunch mint,
    leaves finely chopped
150g/5oz feta cheese, mashed with a fork
olive oil, for shallow-frying
ground black pepper

Courgette and Feta Kyufte

This is a vegetarian version of a Bulgarian favourite, kyufte, or meatballs, which is prepared throughout the year. Grated courgettes are mixed with creamy feta cheese and lots of mint to make small patties that are sautéed in olive oil. Served with a crispy green salad, they are perfect for a summer evening's meal or barbecue.

1 Fry the onion in a pan with the olive oil over medium heat for 5–8 minutes or until it is soft and lightly coloured. Remove, allow to cool, then put into a large bowl.

2 Squeeze the excess moisture from the courgettes and add to the bowl. Combine well.

3 In a separate bowl, beat the egg with the flour until well blended. Season with pepper. Add the mint and mix.

4 Fold the mashed feta cheese into the egg mixture and add to the onion and courgette. Combine.

5 Add a little oil to a heavy, non-stick frying pan and spoon in tablespoons of the courgette mixture, to make a few fritters at a time. Cook on one side for 3–4 minutes, or until set and lightly browned, then turn over and cook the other side for 3–4 minutes, or until browned.

6 Drain the fritters on kitchen paper and keep warm while you cook the remaining fritters.

PER SERVING: Energy 346kcal/1428kJ; Protein 11g; Carbohydrate 10.8g, of which sugars 8.4g; Fat 29g, of which saturates 8.3g; Cholesterol 74mg; Calcium 220mg; Fibre 3g; Sodium 566mg.

Stuffed Courgettes with Pomegranate and Pine Nuts

Courgettes are a variety of summer squash, usually eaten when young and immature, before the seeds are capable of reproducing. Their flesh is firm and watery, the skin shiny and tender. Courgettes are available in different colours; the very pale-green ones and those that are almost white are particularly flavoursome. These are especially popular in Bulgaria and are available in most Turkish or Middle Eastern stores elsewhere. Use the ordinary green courgettes if you can't get hold of the pale-green or white ones.

Serves 4

115g/4oz/1 cup pine nuts
8 pale-green courgettes (zucchini)
30ml/2 tbsp olive oil, plus extra
　for drizzling
1 onion, finely chopped
2 garlic cloves, crushed
2.5ml/½ tsp ground allspice
2.5ml/½ tsp ground cinnamon
185g/6½oz/scant 1 cup long grain rice
seeds of 2 pomegranates
60ml/4 tbsp chopped fresh parsley
salt and ground black pepper
115g/4oz feta cheese, to serve

1 Put the pine nuts in a dry pan and toast over medium-high heat, tossing regularly, for 1–2 minutes, or until golden brown. Set aside. Halve the courgettes lengthways. Using a small sharp knife, carefully hollow them out, removing all the seed pulp from the centre.

2 To make the stuffing, heat the olive oil in a large sauté pan and add the onion, garlic, salt, pepper, allspice and cinnamon. Sauté for 5 minutes, then add the rice and cook for a further 2 minutes, making sure that the rice grains are well coated with the spice mixture.

3 Add 150ml/¼ pint/⅔ cup water and cook until the rice is al dente: tender with a bite in the centre. Remove from the heat, add the pine nuts, pomegranate seeds and parsley, then leave to cool. Preheat the oven to 180°C/350°F/Gas 4.

4 Fill the courgette halves with the stuffing and put into an ovenproof dish. Drizzle with a little olive oil and add about 100ml/3½fl oz/scant ½ cup water to the dish.

5 Bake uncovered for about 30 minutes, or until tender, basting occasionally with the pan juices. Serve with crumbled feta cheese.

COOK'S TIP

When buying courgettes look for smaller, younger courgettes, which will have more flavour, and for firm, heavy courgettes with unblemished and smooth-textured skin.

PER SERVING: Energy 494kcal/2048kJ; Protein 12.4g; Carbohydrate 51.1g, of which sugars 12g; Fat 26.7g, of which saturates 2.3g; Cholesterol 0mg; Calcium 109mg; Fibre 4g; Sodium 10mg.

Bulgarian Aubergine Salad

Serves 4
2 large aubergines (eggplants)
juice of 2 lemons
60ml/4 tbsp olive oil
4 garlic cloves, crushed
75ml/5 tbsp chopped fresh parsley
50g/2oz/⅓ cup walnuts, coarsely chopped
salt and ground black pepper

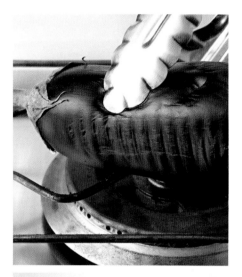

This traditional salad, called kiopolu, has been described as aubergine – or poor man's – caviar. Recipes sometimes include yogurt, tahini or mayonnaise. The key to its success is the smoky flavour of the charred aubergines. Serve with flatbread.

1 If cooking with gas, spear the aubergines with a long-handled fork, or grip with tongs, and hold above the naked flame of the gas ring, turning until the aubergine is charred and soft. If using an electric stove, put the whole aubergine on top of your hot plate and cook, turning, as for gas.

2 Put the cooked aubergines in a colander and leave them to cool.

3 When they are cool enough to handle, peel off the blackened skin and discard. Squeeze the excess water out of the aubergines. Chop the flesh and put into a large bowl.

4 Add the lemon juice, olive oil, garlic, and salt and pepper to taste, mix well and adjust the seasoning. Sprinkle with the parsley and walnuts. Serve cold.

PER SERVING: Energy 210kcal/866kJ; Protein 3.5g; Carbohydrate 3.6g, of which sugars 3.2g; Fat 20.3g, of which saturates 2.4g; Cholesterol 0mg; Calcium 59mg; Fibre 3.8g; Sodium 9mg.

Serves 4

4 long yellow (bell) peppers
4 long green (bell) peppers
60ml/4 tbsp olive oil
2 garlic cloves, crushed
45ml/3 tbsp white wine vinegar
4 plum tomatoes, thinly sliced
1 red onion, thinly sliced
salt and ground black pepper
10 fresh coriander (cilantro) sprigs,
   to garnish

Romanian Grilled Pepper Salad

The Romanians are enormously keen on peppers – which are delicious, flavoursome and abundant when in season. This salad, salata de ardei, is an absolute must on the mezze table and has a tangy taste that makes it an excellent accompaniment to meat. The best peppers to use are the long, sweet variety in green and yellow, but if you can't get hold of these, then round peppers also work well.

1 If cooking with gas, spear the peppers with a long-handled fork and hold directly above the naked flame of the gas ring, turning until the whole pepper is charred and soft. If using an electric stove, put the whole pepper on top of your hot plate and cook, turning, as for gas. This can be done on a barbecue or under a grill (broiler) if you prefer.

2 Put the cooked peppers in a bowl and cover with a dish towel, allowing them to sweat for 10 minutes. This makes peeling them easier. Peel the peppers, discarding the tops and seeds, then slice in long strips and put into a large mixing bowl.

3 Put the olive oil in a bowl and add the garlic and vinegar. Combine into a smooth purée. Season with salt and pepper, and add to the peppers.

4 Add the tomatoes and onion slices to the pepper mixture and combine gently. Adjust the seasoning. Serve garnished with coriander sprigs.

PER SERVING: Energy 254kcal/1057kJ; Protein 5.1g; Carbohydrate 31.1g, of which sugars 28.8g; Fat 12.9g, of which saturates 2g; Cholesterol 0mg; Calcium 50mg; Fibre 7.7g; Sodium 26mg.

Crisp Aubergine, Feta and Caramelized Shallot Salad

This is a modern version of a traditional recipe called salata de vinete, popular in both Romania and Bulgaria. The aubergine and feta combine beautifully and are a well-established pairing. This dish is lovely when served as a light appetizer. For convenience it can be prepared earlier and assembled at the last minute. The salad tastes particularly good with sheep's milk feta cheese, but goat's cheese is an acceptable substitute.

Serves 4

1 medium aubergine (eggplant), unpeeled and thinly sliced
90ml/6 tbsp olive oil
3 shallots, thinly sliced
200g/7oz rocket (arugula) leaves
30ml/2 tbsp balsamic vinegar
115g/4oz sheep's feta cheese, crumbled
salt and ground black pepper
30ml/2 tbsp fresh mint leaves, to garnish

1 Brush each aubergine slice with oil, using about 60ml/4 tbsp.

2 Put a heavy, non-stick frying pan over medium-high heat and, when hot, cook the aubergine slices for about 2 minutes on each side, a few at a time, until golden and crisp. Set aside.

3 To cook the shallots, heat the remaining olive oil in another frying pan. Add the shallots and cook over medium heat to caramelize them. This will take about 6–8 minutes.

4 Put the rocket in a bowl and toss with the balsamic vinegar, then season to taste. Divide between four serving plates. Put some crisp aubergine on top of each, then add some crumbled feta, finishing with the caramelized shallots and some mint leaves.

COOK'S TIP
The secret of this dish is to cook the aubergines with as little oil as possible so that they are compact and crispy when served.

PER SERVING: Energy 246kcal/1014kJ; Protein 6.5g; Carbohydrate 3.5g, of which sugars 3g; Fat 22.9g, of which saturates 6.4g; Cholesterol 20mg; Calcium 197mg; Fibre 2.3g; Sodium 486mg.

Serves 4

4 ripe plum tomatoes, diced
½ cucumber, diced
1 long green (bell) pepper,
  seeded and diced
1 red onion, thinly sliced
60ml/4 tbsp olive oil
45ml/3 tbsp white wine vinegar
1 small bunch parsley, leaves
  finely chopped
150g/5oz feta cheese, crumbled
salt and ground black pepper

Shopska Salata

This is the best-known and best-loved dish in Bulgaria, named after the village folk around Sofia, who are known as *shopi*. This salad is fresh, crisp, full of delicious vegetables and topped with crumbled creamy feta cheese. Salads in Bulgaria are eaten as appetizers or served to accompany a main dish.

1 Put the prepared tomatoes, cucumber, pepper and onion into a large bowl.

2 Season the ingredients in the bowl with pepper and a little salt – be careful not to add too much salt as the feta is naturally salty.

3 Put the olive oil and vinegar in a jug (pitcher) and mix well.

4 Add the oil and vinegar to the vegetables. Add the parsley and toss all the ingredients gently to combine them. Top the salad with the feta cheese and serve.

PER SERVING: Energy 232kcal/959kJ; Protein 7.6g; Carbohydrate 7.6g, of which sugars 7g; Fat 19.2g, of which saturates 6.8g; Cholesterol 26mg; Calcium 177mg; Fibre 2.4g; Sodium 554mg.

Bulgarian Yogurt Salad

This yogurt salad is extremely popular in the hot summer months. Called suh (dry) tarator, it is made from strained thick yogurt and fresh cucumber, and has the same ingredients as the chilled tarator soup. The salad is similar to the Greek tzatziki, but walnuts added as a garnish give the traditional recipe a slight twist. The salad is also called Sneganka, after the Bulgarian Snow White.

1 Peel the cucumber and dice finely (or grate, if you prefer).

2 Put the cucumber into a bowl and add the yogurt, garlic and mint. Season to taste with salt and pepper and combine well.

3 Spoon on to serving plates, drizzle with the olive oil and sprinkle with the chopped walnuts.

4 Refrigerate for several hours before serving with crackers, pitta bread or crusty bread of your choice.

Serves 4
1 cucumber
300g/11oz/scant 1½ cups Greek
   (US strained plain) yogurt
2 garlic cloves, crushed
15ml/1 tbsp chopped fresh mint
30ml/2 tbsp olive oil
30ml/2 tbsp chopped walnuts, to garnish
salt and ground black pepper

PER SERVING: Energy 194kcal/801kJ; Protein 6.4g; Carbohydrate 2.7g, of which sugars 2.4g; Fat 18.4g, of which saturates 5.1g; Cholesterol 0mg; Calcium 137mg; Fibre 0.6g; Sodium 56mg.

SOUPS & HOTPOTS

One-pot meals and soups that simmer gently on the stove to create delicious, satisfying combinations are a strong tradition in Romania and Bulgaria. Cast-iron kettles, ceramic casseroles and clay vessels are used, enabling the gradual infusion of flavours throughout the container. Dishes to keep the cold at bay include chorba, a nourishing vegetable and meat soup, and a flavoursome hotpot from Bucharest with potatoes, smoked sausage and whatever lentils, beans and peas you might have to hand.

Warming chorba to cool tarator

Soups and hotpot dishes have a coveted place in Bulgarian and Romanian kitchens, and most meals will feature one or the other. Stock cubes are not widely used, even today, so home-made soups generally use their own stocks, giving them an extra freshness. Hot soups are always a welcome winter warmer, with chorba or ciorba a particular favourite, often made with lentils or beans. Lamb and cabbage (fresh or preserved) often feature in Bulgarian soups. There are also many recipes for fruit soups based on seasonal produce, for example apricots, apples, gooseberries and plums; here the ingredients are often left unpuréed. In summer, chilled soups are great favourites, with the Bulgarian tarator, a cooling, yogurt-based cucumber soup, a delicious example.

Traditionally, many soups were prepared for medicinal purposes, with ingredients selected to treat individual ailments. Soup made of preserved cabbage or sauerkraut was believed to be an effective hangover cure, and chicken soup is still used as a remedy for a light cold or a sore throat.

Soups are often served as a separate course following the mezze table, and would normally be accompanied with fresh crusty bread. Diners should remember to pace themselves at this point in the meal as there is a substantial main course still to follow.

Serves 4

45ml/3 tbsp olive oil

1 large onion, finely chopped

3 garlic cloves, finely chopped

50g/2oz/¼ cup ready-to-eat dried
   apricots, chopped

300g/11oz/scant 1½ cups split red
   lentils

1 litre/1¾ pints/4 cups vegetable stock
   or water

3 medium tomatoes, peeled and
   chopped, or use canned tomatoes

2.5ml/½ tsp ground cumin

handful of thyme leaves

juice of 1 lemon

salt and ground black pepper

handful of flat leaf parsley,
   leaves chopped, to garnish

Lentil and Apricot Soup

This soup is delightfully light and elegant. Lentils are excellent soup components, but are also used for stuffing, in salads and in terrines. Dried apricots are a Turkish touch that blend beautifully with the red lentils. The soup is bright orange and almost luminous when cooked.

1 Heat the oil in a large, heavy pan over medium heat. Add the onion, garlic and dried apricots. Sauté, stirring, for 10 minutes, or until the onions are soft. Add the lentils and stock, and bring to the boil.

2 Reduce the heat, cover and simmer for 20–30 minutes, or until the lentils are soft and tender.

3 Add the tomatoes, cumin and thyme, and simmer for a further 15 minutes.

4 Spoon the soup into a food processor or blender and purée in batches until smooth. Return the purée to the pan and add the lemon juice, salt and pepper to taste. Sprinkle liberally with the parsley, and serve hot.

COOK'S TIP

To peel the tomatoes easily, plunge them into boiling water for 30 seconds, then refresh in cold water. Peel away the skins.

PER SERVING: Energy 377kcal/1589kJ; Protein 20.2g; Carbohydrate 55.4g, of which sugars 13.2g; Fat 9.8g, of which saturates 1.4g; Cholesterol 0mg; Calcium 97mg; Fibre 6.9g; Sodium 42mg.

Serves 4

2 medium cucumbers, peeled
500ml/17fl oz/2¼ cups Greek
  (US strained plain) yogurt
1 small garlic clove, crushed
handful of fresh mint leaves
olive oil, for drizzling
salt and ground black pepper
40g/1½oz/3 tbsp walnuts, chopped,
  to garnish

Tarator

Tarator is classic cold yogurt soup with cucumber, rather like the salad suh tarator (see page 51). This soup originates in Turkey, but this version is Bulgarian. The fresh combination of flavours makes it an ideal prelude to a main course.

1 Halve the cucumbers lengthways, and scoop out the seeds from the centre, then dice them finely.

2 Whisk the yogurt with 250ml/ 8fl oz/1 cup water until smooth. Season to taste with salt and pepper. Add the cucumbers to the yogurt and stir well.

3 Add the garlic and mint leaves, and leave to stand for 10 minutes. Serve with a drizzle of olive oil and a sprinkling of chopped walnuts on top.

SERVING SUGGESTION

Tarator is delicious when served with a chunky slice of crusty wholemeal (whole-wheat) bread and feta cheese.

PER SERVING: Energy 272kcal/1123kJ; Protein 10.2g; Carbohydrate 4.3g, of which sugars 4.2g; Fat 25.2g, of which saturates 7.8g; Cholesterol 0mg; Calcium 215mg; Fibre 1g; Sodium 93mg.

Kohlrabi, Apple and Caraway Soup

Romanians are very keen on fruit soups, especially during the summer when the fruit harvest is at its height. This kohlrabi soup with apples, supa de gulie mere şi chimion, is absolutely delicious, having a delightfully sweet edge. For an authentic Romanian style, serve the soup with the ingredients left chunky and unpuréed. Other fruits and berries used as soup components include apricot, cherry, plum, gooseberries and redcurrants; depending on their preparation they can have a savoury emphasis or a much sweeter one.

Serves 4–6
10g/¼oz/½ tbsp butter
1 kohlrabi, diced
2 carrots, diced
2 celery sticks, diced
1 yellow (bell) pepper, seeded and diced
1 tomato, diced
1.5 litres/2½ pints/6¼ cups
    vegetable stock
800g/1¾lb crisp, green eating
    apples, peeled
15ml/1 tbsp sugar
2.5ml/½ tsp ground caraway seeds
45ml/3 tbsp sour cream
1 small bunch parsley, leaves chopped
salt and ground black pepper

1 Put the butter in a large pan and melt over medium heat. Add the diced vegetables and sauté for 3–4 minutes, or until soft. Season to taste.

2 Add the vegetable stock and bring to the boil, then reduce the heat to low and simmer for 1 hour.

3 Grate the apples and add to the simmering soup, followed by the sugar and the caraway seeds. Cook for a further 15 minutes and adjust the seasoning.

4 Stir in the sour cream and sprinkle with the parsley. Serve hot.

COOK'S TIPS
• Kohlrabi survives frost very well and can be stored over a long period in a suitable cool, dark storage area.
• Kohlrabi bulbs are available in white and purple varieties – the white ones have much more flavour when they are small. Purple kohlrabi tends to have a spicier taste.
• If your kohlrabi arrives with the green tops intact they can be prepared as greens. Blanch them until just wilted and peel off the leaves from the tough main stem. Drain and squeeze excess water from the leaves. Chop the leaves and combine with a little olive oil. Season with salt and pepper and add a small amount of fresh lemon juice.

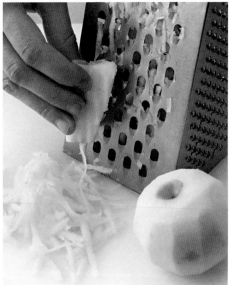

Serves 6

45ml/3 tbsp olive oil

2 ripe tomatoes, chopped

3 garlic cloves, crushed

1 onion, finely chopped

2 celery sticks, finely chopped

1 carrot, finely chopped

300g/11oz/1⅔ cups dried haricot (navy)
    beans, soaked overnight,
    drained and rinsed

5ml/1 tsp sweet paprika

2.5ml/½ tsp hot paprika

1.2 litres/2 pints/5 cups
    chicken stock

1 small bunch parsley,
    leaves finely chopped

salt and ground black pepper

Haricot Bean Soup

This bean soup, fasul chorba, is almost a national dish in Bulgaria, and you can find different versions at small eateries around the mountainous countryside. Prepared in monasteries around the country at Easter, it is also known as monastery soup. You can use any white beans, but the best flavour is achieved using haricot beans.

1 Put the oil in a large pan over medium heat. Add the tomatoes, garlic, onion, celery and carrot.

2 Sauté the contents of the pan for 5 minutes, stirring constantly. Season to taste with salt and pepper.

3 Add the drained beans, and the sweet and hot paprika. Pour in the stock and simmer for 1½ hours, or until the beans are soft. Add the parsley and serve hot.

COOK'S TIP

It is always advisable to use dry beans prepared as shown above, but if you don't have adequate preparation time then you can use cans of haricot beans. In this case you will need to reduce the cooking time at step 3 to half an hour.

VARIATION

As an alternative, serve with a dollop of yogurt, chopped mint and fresh bread.

PER SERVING: Energy 204kcal/859kJ; Protein 12.1g; Carbohydrate 25.3g, of which sugars 3.7g; Fat 6.7g, of which saturates 1g; Cholesterol 0mg; Calcium 83mg; Fibre 9.1g; Sodium 24mg.

Serves 4

1 litre/1¾ pints/4 cups chicken stock

2 large potatoes, peeled and grated

1 large carrot, grated

30ml/2 tbsp natural (plain) yogurt

1 egg yolk

30ml/2 tbsp lemon juice

45ml/3 tbsp finely chopped fresh parsley,
   to garnish

For the meatballs

1 large slice crusty bread, crust removed

200g/7oz/scant 1 cup minced (ground) veal

200g/7oz/scant 1 cup minced (ground) pork

½ onion, finely chopped

15ml/1 tbsp plain (all-purpose) flour

salt and ground black pepper

Bulgarian Meatball Soup

This one-pot-meal soup, supa topcheta, has a long history and would have been a regular supper for many families. It has strong Turkish influences, which is no surprise, as Turkey ruled Bulgaria for almost 500 years. It is quick to make because the meatballs are cooked in the soup broth instead of being browned separately.

1 To make the meatballs, soak the bread in water, then squeeze out the excess liquid. Put the minced veal and pork into a bowl and add the bread and onion. Season and mix well until the mixture holds together.

2 Shape the mixture into small balls, about 2cm/¾in in diameter. Roll in the flour and shake off the excess.

3 Put the chicken stock in a large pan and bring to the boil.

4 Drop in the meatballs and add the grated potatoes and carrot. Simmer for 20 minutes, or until the meatballs are cooked through.

5 Meanwhile, put the yogurt into a small bowl and mix in the egg yolk and lemon juice. Stir some of the soup liquid into this mixture, and then pour the mixture into the soup. Mix well and heat through briefly. Sprinkle the soup with parsley and serve hot.

PER SERVING: Energy 294kcal/1236kJ; Protein 23.2g; Carbohydrate 25.6g, of which sugars 4.3g; Fat 11.7g, of which saturates 4.2g; Cholesterol 117mg; Calcium 54mg; Fibre 1.9g; Sodium 126mg.

Serves 6
30ml/2 tbsp olive oil
1 onion, finely chopped
300g/11oz pork shoulder, cubed
500g/1¼lb sauerkraut
500ml/17fl oz/generous 2 cups chicken
   stock
5ml/1 tsp paprika
2.5ml/½ tsp ground caraway seeds
300g/11oz smoked pork sausage, cubed
salt and ground black pepper

Sauerkraut, Pork and Caraway Soup

This soup, ciorba de varza ăcra și chimiou, can typically be found on menus all over Romania during the cold winter months, as it is a substantial, nourishing and comforting meal. It has a slightly sour flavour from the fermented sauerkraut. Serve with rye bread.

1 Put the olive oil in a pan with the onion and sauté over medium heat for 5 minutes, or until just softened.

2 Add the pork and sauté for 5–8 minutes.

3 Drain the sauerkraut into a bowl. Measure out 500ml/17fl oz/generous 2 cups of the liquid and reserve. Finely chop the sauerkraut.

4 Add the sauerkraut to the pan with the measured liquid and the stock.

5 Bring to the boil and reduce the heat to a simmer. Add the paprika and caraway, then cover and simmer over a low heat for 35 minutes.

6 Season to taste and stir in the smoked sausage. Continue cooking for a further 30 minutes. Serve hot.

VARIATION

This soup recipe can also be adapted to work as a more filling one-pot meal. Just add some peeled, chopped potatoes at step 4 and cook them with the sauerkraut.

PER SERVING: Energy 296kcal/1227kJ; Protein 17.4g; Carbohydrate 7.3g, of which sugars 2.2g; Fat 22.1g, of which saturates 7.4g; Cholesterol 55mg; Calcium 73mg; Fibre 2.2g; Sodium 908mg.

Serves 4–6

1.5 litres/2½ pints/6¼ cups veal stock

400g/14oz/2¼ cups chickpeas, soaked overnight, drained and rinsed

1 large potato, peeled and coarsely grated

1 large carrot, coarsely grated

300g/11oz fresh chard leaves or other greens, roughly chopped

150g/5oz smoked sausage, peeled and thinly sliced

salt and ground black pepper

Bucharest Hotpot

This delicious hotpot, gulaş de Bucureşti, is traditionally prepared with whatever beans and peas are to hand. Chickpeas have a nutty flavour that works well, but it can also be made with beans. Thin slices of smoked sausage are added at the end of cooking. Serve with crusty bread.

1 Put the veal stock in a large pan and bring to the boil over medium heat. Add the chickpeas, bring to the boil and cook for 1 hour.

2 Add the grated potato and carrot, season with salt and pepper and simmer for a further 15 minutes.

3 Add the chopped chard leaves or greens and sliced sausage, then remove from the heat. Serve hot.

COOK'S TIP

Use any type of smoked sausage that you can find, but a quality Polish variety is a good option.

PER SERVING: Energy 359kcal/1508kJ; Protein 19.2g; Carbohydrate 45.6g, of which sugars 4.7g; Fat 12.2g, of which saturates 3.5g; Cholesterol 12mg; Calcium 209mg; Fibre 9.2g; Sodium 296mg.

Mutton Hotpot

Although mutton is still loved all over Bulgaria, this dish that was once so popular can now be found only in the most remote regions. Locally it's called kurban chorba, the word chorba meaning 'soup' in both Bulgarian and Turkish; this dish does in fact have its roots in Turkish cuisine, just like many other Bulgarian dishes.

Serves 6

2 litres/3½ pints/9 cups lamb stock
300g/11oz lean mutton or lamb, diced
150g/5oz lamb's liver, diced
30ml/2 tbsp olive oil
1 large onion, finely chopped
3 rosemary sprigs, leaves finely chopped
5 thyme sprigs, leaves finely chopped
1 bay leaf
15ml/1 tbsp cornflour (cornstarch)
1 large ripe tomato, diced
5ml/1 tsp sweet paprika
1 large egg, beaten
1 small bunch parsley, finely chopped,
 to garnish
salt and ground black pepper

1 Put the stock in a large pan and bring to the boil. Add the mutton or lamb and simmer for 45–50 minutes. Skim off the scum occasionally as it cooks.

2 Add the liver to the pan and cook for a further 20 minutes. Season to taste. Strain the cooking liquid into a bowl and keep the meat separate.

3 Using the same pan, heat the olive oil and then add the onion, rosemary, thyme and bay leaf, and sauté for 3–4 minutes.

4 Add the cornflour and stir to create a smooth roux. Gradually add the reserved cooking liquid, stirring the sauce constantly.

5 Add the tomato, the meat and sweet paprika. Simmer over low heat for 8–10 minutes.

6 Add some of the hot soup to the beaten egg and combine well. Pour into the pan and stir well. Adjust the seasoning, sprinkle with the parsley, and serve the dish hot.

COOK'S TIPS

• While traditionally the main meat component of this hotpot is mutton, spring lamb combines well with mutton or can be used as the main ingredient. This will make the dish lighter and give it a more tender texture.
• Diced mutton is normally cut from the shoulder and is an ideal ingredient for meat casseroles, curries, tagines and pies.
• To make mutton more tender and to improve the flavour, you can rub the uncooked meat with vinegar and marinate for about 20 minutes before rinsing well.

PER SERVING: Energy 217kcal/906kJ; Protein 16.9g; Carbohydrate 8.7g, of which sugars 4.2g; Fat 12g, of which saturates 4.1g; Cholesterol 177mg; Calcium 30mg; Fibre 1.1g; Sodium 79mg.

FISH & SEAFOOD

With so much surrounding sea, endless rivers and lakes and a shared tradition of fishing for food and for pleasure, the menus of Bulgaria and Romania include both freshwater and saltwater fish. During the winter months when supplies of fresh fish are reduced, frozen fish is widely available. Dishes in this chapter are baked, fried and marinated. They include the melt-in-your mouth sweetness of trout and carp, the crunchy taste of fried whitebait and the silky clean texture of seabass stuffed with creamy feta and herbs.

From the Danube to the Black Sea

With coastlines adjacent to the Black Sea, Bulgaria and Romania benefit from a plentiful variety of sea fish. Often used in Bulgaria is a regional variety of turbot called kalkan, as well as sea bass and whitebait. There is also a huge variety of river fish, sourced from rivers and lakes all over the mountain regions. These include trout, particularly delicious when in season, pike, perch and carp. Bulgarian recipes in this chapter include the festive Carp Stuffed with Walnuts and Golden Spices, and Cod Plaki, a light summer casserole baked with seasonal vegetables.

In Romania, too, from the Black Sea coast, the River Danube and countless smaller rivers and lakes comes a good supply of fish. Sturgeon, trout, carp, pike, perch and bream are baked or grilled and often made into stews.

Although sturgeon is popular, it has been been overfished for its caviar in the Danube Delta and is now classed as an endangered species, so it doesn't appear as an ingredient here. There are a number of fish species under threat, so take care to use sustainable sources. Atlantic cod, white hake and Atlantic octopus, for example, are in short supply, so use alternatives such as Alaska pollock or Pacific cod; silver or red hake and Pacific halibut; and Pacific octopus. Advice is also available from organizations such as the World Wildlife Fund and the Environmental Defense Fund (see Useful Addresses on page 126).

Serves 4
5ml/1 tsp caraway seeds
15g/½oz/1 tbsp butter
4 carp fillets, about 185g/6½oz each
6 fresh dill sprigs, finely chopped
100ml/3½fl oz/scant ½ cup white wine
50ml/2fl oz/¼ cup extra-thick double
    (heavy) cream
5ml/1 tsp horseradish cream
200g/7oz green beans
salt and ground black pepper

Carp with Dill and Horseradish Sauce

Carp is plentiful in Romania and it features in many local recipes. This one, crap cu sos marar şi hrean, is from the Danube region where the carp is fished straight from the river. This dish also works well with cod or haddock.

1 Put the caraway seeds in a dry pan and toast over medium-high heat, tossing regularly, for 1 minute.

2 Crush the seeds using a mortar and pestle. Melt the butter in a large frying pan over medium-high heat and add the carp fillets. Cook for 1 minute on each side.

3 Reduce the heat and add the caraway seeds, dill and wine.

4 Cook the fish for 5–8 minutes, or until the fish is cooked through, then add the cream and horseradish cream. Season to taste.

5 Meanwhile, bring a small pan of water to the boil and drop in the green beans. Cook for 3 minutes until crisp-tender. Drain. Serve the carp with the dill and horseradish sauce, accompanied by the crunchy green beans.

PER SERVING: Energy 310kcal/1295kJ; Protein 31.9g; Carbohydrate 2.3g, of which sugars 1.8g; Fat 18.4g, of which saturates 7.4g; Cholesterol 142mg; Calcium 110mg; Fibre 1.1g; Sodium 120mg.

Serves 4

6 large, long sweet red (bell) peppers
30ml/2 tbsp olive oil
2 red onions, sliced
4 large fillets of carp, skinned
115g/4oz pancetta, thinly sliced
  into strips
30 sage leaves
65g/2½oz/5 tbsp butter
1.5ml/¼ tsp paprika
sour cream to serve (optional)

Carp with Pancetta and Sage

The traditional way to cook carp is whole, stuffed with fruits and nuts and then baked. This Romanian recipe for carp stuffed with strips of pancetta and sage, crap cu sunculiţă şi salvie, has been modernized and adapted to Western tastes. Carp is a common part of the diet across Eastern Europe, and in Poland it forms the base of their Christmas dinner.

1 Preheat the oven to 200°C/400°F/ Gas 6. Arrange the long red peppers in a roasting pan and roast in the oven for 25 minutes. Cool and remove the skins and seeds. Slice into thin strips.

2 Heat the olive oil in a large pan and sauté the onions for 5–7 minutes, or until just transparent. Remove the pan from the heat, add the peppers and keep warm.

3 Make cuts into the flesh of each carp fillet and stuff with pancetta strips and sage leaves.

4 Melt the butter in a small pan and stir in the paprika. Brush this mixture on to each fillet. Arrange the fish on a baking tray and bake for 20–30 minutes, or until the fish is cooked.

5 Serve the carp accompanied by the peppers and red onions.

PER SERVING: Energy 640kcal/2661kJ; Protein 43.8g; Carbohydrate 24.5g, of which sugars 21.4g; Fat 41.4g, of which saturates 17.3g; Cholesterol 205mg; Calcium 158mg; Fibre 5.4g; Sodium 610mg.

Carp Stuffed with Walnuts and Golden Spices

Pulnen sharan is a spectacular festive dish that makes a regular appearance at Christmas on many dinner tables in Bulgaria. Carp is a common river fish there and it is quite normal to catch individual fish as large as 15kg/33lb. Freshwater fish are just as nutritious as saltwater fish; they contain the same amount of the essential mineral phosphorus as well as the same level of easily digestible proteins. Carp has a very soft and sweet flesh and the larger ones have much fewer bones. If you can't find carp, salmon is another suitable fish to use when preparing this recipe.

Serves 8–10

1 large carp, about 1.5–2kg/3¼–4½lb, cleaned, gutted and descaled
60ml/4 tbsp extra virgin olive oil, plus extra for drizzling
6 large onions, thinly sliced
1.5ml/¼ tsp ground cumin
1.5ml/¼ tsp ground cinnamon
5ml/1 tsp paprika
300g/11oz/scant 2 cups walnuts, ground coarsely
115g/4oz/scant 1 cup sultanas (golden raisins)
1 bunch parsley, leaves finely chopped
salt and ground black pepper
1 lemon, sliced into wedges, to serve (optional)

1 Preheat the oven to 180°C/350°F/Gas 4. Prepare and lightly oil an oval dish large enough to hold the carp. Wash the fish well, then dry with kitchen paper. Season with salt and pepper, and put into the dish.

2 Put the olive oil into a large, deep pan and add the onions. Cook gently for 10–12 minutes, or until just golden.

3 Add the spices, walnuts, sultanas and parsley to the pan. Stir in well and remove from the heat.

4 Stuff the carp belly with the mixture. Secure the opening with cocktail sticks (toothpicks). Add any leftover stuffing to the dish.

5 Drizzle the fish with a little olive oil and bake for 1 hour. Serve with boiled potatoes, crispy greens and a tomato salad.

PER SERVING: Energy 429kcal/1783kJ; Protein 23.6g; Carbohydrate 17.2g, of which sugars 14.5g; Fat 30g, of which saturates 3.2g; Cholesterol 67mg; Calcium 119mg; Fibre 2.9g; Sodium 52mg.

Trout Baked in White Wine with Buttered Almonds

Sweet-flavoured, white-fleshed trout is commonly eaten in Bulgaria and Romania and tastes wonderful when it is baked. This recipe, in Romania păstrăv cu alune la cuptor, works with whatever trout is available.

Serves 4

4 trout, about 200g/7oz each, cleaned and descaled, head on
1 red onion, sliced into rings
300ml/½ pint/1¼ cups white wine
2 bay leaves
2–3 sprigs each of fresh parsley, thyme and rosemary
4–5 black peppercorns
½ lemon, cut into wedges
15g/½oz/1 tbsp butter
45ml/3 tbsp flaked (sliced) almonds
salt and ground black pepper

1 Preheat the oven to 180°C/350°F/Gas 4. Season the trout and put on a baking tray. Place the onions inside the fish and pour over the wine. Add the bay leaves, herbs, peppercorns and lemon wedges to the tray. Cover the tray with foil. Bake for 30 minutes.

2 Take out of the oven and carefully remove the foil, making sure that you do not scald yourself with the escaping steam. Keep the fish warm and pour the cooking liquid into a small pan.

3 Put the pan over medium-high heat and cook for 5–8 minutes to reduce the liquid slightly. Adjust the seasoning.

4 Meanwhile, melt the butter in a small pan and add the almonds. Cook for 3–4 minutes, or until the almonds are golden and crispy.

5 Serve the trout with the almonds on top, accompanied by the reduced cooking juices.

PER SERVING: Energy 347kcal/1453kJ; Protein 34.1g; Carbohydrate 2.4g, of which sugars 1.8g; Fat 17.2g, of which saturates 4.2g; Cholesterol 111mg; Calcium 68mg; Fibre 1.1g; Sodium 113mg.

Serves 6
vegetable oil, for deep-frying
500g/1¼lb whitebait, washed
60ml/4 tbsp plain (all-purpose) flour
salt and ground black pepper
4 lemons, cut into wedges, to serve

For the garlic sauce
2 garlic cloves, crushed
30ml/2 tbsp mayonnaise
100ml/3½fl oz/scant ½ cup yogurt

Fried Whitebait with Garlic Sauce

Whitebait is sold in many cafés and delicatessens in Bulgaria. It makes an affordable dish that is truly delicious when prepared well. This typical seaside snack, called zaza, is a firm favourite. It is always served with plenty of lemon juice, but here it is also served with a punchy garlic sauce. It can also be accompanied by garlic mayonnaise.

1 Prepare a large deep-fat fryer or a pan with oil and heat slowly to 180°C (test by frying a small cube of bread; it should brown in 40 seconds). Make sure that the oil does not smoke and do not leave unattended. Pat the fish completely dry with kitchen paper.

2 Put the flour on a plate and add salt and pepper. Add the fish and roll in the flour to coat well.

3 Fry the fish in batches so that it cooks easily and comes out golden and crispy. Keep warm.

4 To make the garlic sauce, put the garlic into a small bowl with the mayonnaise and yogurt. Mix well. Season with salt and pepper. Serve the whitebait with lemon wedges and the garlic sauce.

VARIATION

Chop up a selection of fresh herbs finely and combine with the flour that will be used to coat the fish. Use this mixture in step 2 to cover the whitebait before frying them at step 3.

PER SERVING: Energy 481kcal/1993kJ; Protein 17.2g; Carbohydrate 5.8g, of which sugars 1.4g; Fat 43.5g, of which saturates 0.6g; Cholesterol 4mg; Calcium 749mg; Fibre 0.2g; Sodium 228mg.

Cod Plaki

Plaki is a Greek and Bulgarian method of baking fish. It produces the perfect summer fish dish, cooked with a selection of wonderful, seasonal vegetables. This recipe uses cod, but it is equally good with monkfish, sea bass, red snapper or salmon.

Serves 4

600g/1lb 5oz cod fillet, skinned and small bones removed
90ml/6 tbsp olive oil
2 onions, chopped
3 garlic cloves, chopped
300g/11oz fresh plum tomatoes, chopped
100ml/3½fl oz/scant ½ cup dry white wine
115g/4oz/1 cup green olives, pitted
115g/4oz spinach, chopped
65g/2½oz/scant ½ cup walnuts, coarsely chopped
salt and ground black pepper
75ml/5 tbsp each chopped fresh parsley and basil, to garnish
basmati rice, to serve

1 Cut the fish fillet into 5cm/2in chunks. Put the oil in a deep flameproof casserole, add the onions and garlic, and sauté for 5–8 minutes, or until soft and light golden, but not browned.

2 Add the tomatoes, wine and 100ml/3½fl oz/scant ½ cup water to the casserole. Bring to the boil, then reduce the heat and simmer for a further 10 minutes. The cooking liquid will be slightly reduced at this point, to about half the original quantity. Preheat the oven to 180°C/350°F/Gas 4.

3 Stir in the whole olives and spinach, then arrange the cod pieces on top. Season and simmer for 8 minutes.

4 Add the walnuts to the casserole. Cover and then transfer to the preheated oven and cook for a further 15 minutes. Serve the plaki with the rice, sprinkled with the herbs.

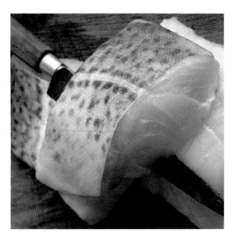

VARIATIONS
• Other vegetables that could easily be combined with this dish at step 2 include sliced courgettes (zucchini), a red (bell) pepper, cut into small cubes, or sliced fresh mushrooms.
• 150g/5oz/1 cup of raisins and 65g/2½oz/½ cup of currants, added along with the vegetables, gives the dish a fruity, more textured quality.
• To serve as a one-pot meal, add peeled and sliced potatoes at step 4, at the same time as adding the walnuts. This makes it a filling, nutritious meal that needs no other accompaniment.
• This recipe can also be served with fresh, crusty bread.

PER SERVING: Energy 491kcal/2038kJ; Protein 33g; Carbohydrate 13.4g, of which sugars 10.3g; Fat 32.5g, of which saturates 4g; Cholesterol 69mg; Calcium 134mg; Fibre 4.5g; Sodium 790mg.

Sea Bass Stuffed with Feta and Herbs

Serves 4

4 medium sea bass, cleaned, gutted, head removed
juice of 1 lemon
50g/2oz/1 cup fresh breadcrumbs
65g/2½oz feta cheese, crumbled
1 egg white
6 tarragon sprigs, leaves finely chopped
6 thyme sprigs, leaves chopped
8 parsley sprigs, leaves finely chopped
50g/2oz/4 tbsp butter, melted
salt and ground black pepper
lemon wedges, to serve

Bulgaria has an extensive Black Sea coastline, but sea fish are only widely eaten in the coastal areas; people living inland prefer freshwater fish. You may find the combination of dairy and fish a little unusual, but this is a fairly typical recipe in the kitchens of Bulgaria.

1 Preheat the oven to 180°C/350°F/ Gas 4. Make sure that the fish fillets are cleaned well, washed and dried with kitchen paper. Rub with the lemon juice and season with salt and pepper.

2 Put the breadcrumbs, feta cheese, egg white and herbs in a bowl and mix well to combine.

3 Spoon some of the filling into the cavity of each fish, then secure with cocktail sticks (toothpicks) and put on to a baking tray.

4 Brush with the melted butter, season with a little salt and pepper and bake for 45–50 minutes, or until cooked through. Serve with lemon wedges.

COOK'S TIP

You can prepare the fish for baking up to 8 hours ahead. Just keep it loosely wrapped in clear film (plastic wrap) in the refrigerator.

PER SERVING: Energy 348kcal/1456kJ; Protein 33.7g; Carbohydrate 9.9g, of which sugars 0.6g; Fat 19.5g, of which saturates 10.9g; Cholesterol 166mg; Calcium 273mg; Fibre 0.3g; Sodium 560mg.

Serves 4

10ml/2 tsp caraway seeds
2 fillets of hake, about 500g/1¼lb each,
  small bones removed
50g/2oz/4 tbsp butter, melted
2.5ml/½ tsp ground fennel seeds
2.5ml/½ tsp ground juniper berries
juice of 1 large lemon
15ml/1 tbsp finely chopped tarragon, to
  garnish
salt and ground black pepper
lemon wedges, to serve

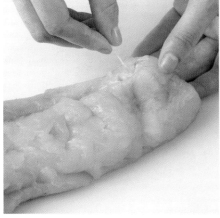

Baked Hake

Hake is a popular fish in Romania, and this recipe, merluciu la cuptor, is perfect as a simple, everyday dish. The recipe also tastes good using cod or salmon. Serve accompanied by a fresh tomato salad and fluffy rice.

1 Preheat the oven to a temperature of 180°C/350°F /Gas 4. Put the caraway seeds in a dry pan and toast over medium-high heat, tossing regularly, for 1 minute, or until the aroma is released.

2 Crush the caraway seeds using a mortar and pestle.

3 Arrange the hake fillets in a roasting pan and drizzle with the butter.

4 Sprinkle with the caraway and fennel seeds and juniper berries, add the lemon juice and season with salt and pepper.

5 Bake for 20–25 minutes. Garnish with tarragon and serve with lemon wedges.

PER SERVING: Energy 212kcal/880kJ; Protein 23g; Carbohydrate 0.4g, of which sugars 0.3g; Fat 13.1g, of which saturates 7.1g; Cholesterol 58mg; Calcium 45mg; Fibre 0.6g; Sodium 223mg.

Serves 4
8 pike steaks, about 150g/5oz each
45ml/3 tbsp melted butter
50ml/2fl oz/¼ cup white wine
100ml/3½fl oz/scant ½ cup fish stock
salt and ground black pepper

For the marinade
75ml/2½fl oz/⅓ cup white wine vinegar
75ml/2½fl oz/⅓ cup fish stock
4 juniper berries, crushed
5 allspice berries, crushed
5ml/1 tsp onion seeds
½ onion, sliced
2 garlic cloves, crushed
1 bay leaf
5 thyme sprigs
5 dill sprigs

Romanian Marinated Pike

Pike is fished all over Romania, but the tastiest variety comes from the Danube. In this dish, ştiucă marinată, the cooked fish soaks in a fruity and spicy marinade to give it a rich flavour. Serve with salads and rye bread.

1 Preheat the oven to 180°C/350°F/ Gas 4. Arrange the pike steaks next to each other in a large ovenproof dish, brush with the melted butter, then pour in the wine and stock. Season to taste.

2 Bake the fish for 25 minutes, or until lightly browned. Remove from the oven and allow the fish to cool completely in the cooking juices. Carefully spoon off the cooking juices and reserve.

3 To make the marinade, put all the ingredients, except for the thyme and dill, in a pan with the reserved cooking juices from the fish. Adjust the seasoning to taste.

4 Bring to the boil, and then reduce the heat and simmer for 20 minutes. Wait until cool.

5 Pour the marinade over the fish and add the thyme and dill sprigs. Cover and put in the refrigerator overnight. Serve cold.

PER SERVING: Energy 212kcal/880kJ; Protein 23g; Carbohydrate 0.4g, of which sugars 0.3g; Fat 13.1g, of which saturates 7.1g; Cholesterol 58mg; Calcium 45mg; Fibre 0.6g; Sodium 223mg.

Serves 6

900g/2lb baby octopus, washed
 and cleaned
45ml/3 tbsp extra virgin olive oil
1 fennel bulb, trimmed and sliced into
 paper-thin slices
6 cherry tomatoes, halved
200g/7oz lamb's lettuce
salt and ground black pepper

For the dressing
60ml/4 tbsp extra virgin olive oil
45ml/3 tbsp lemon juice
5ml/1 tsp made mustard
2.5ml/½ tsp honey
salt and ground black pepper

Octopus and Fennel Salad

This light, modern salad can also be prepared using squid and is perfect for the extremely hot Bulgarian summers. While not a traditional dish, this is a popular choice among young Bulgarians.

1 Bring a large pan of water to the boil. Add a little salt and drop in the octopus. Cook for 20–25 minutes, until soft. Make sure that you do not overcook the octopus or it will become tough and rubbery. Remove the octopus with a slotted spoon; discard the water. Cut the tentacles from the body and head, and slice thinly. Put into a bowl.

2 Add 45ml/3 tbsp of olive oil to a frying pan and sauté the fennel for 5–7 minutes. Season to taste.

3 Allow to cool and transfer into the bowl with the octopus. Add the cherry tomatoes and lettuce and gently mix together.

4 To make the dressing, whisk all the ingredients together and pour over the octopus salad.

5 Toss the salad gently to combine the dressing, season to taste and serve in deep serving plates.

PER SERVING: Energy 268kcal/1118kJ; Protein 27.5g; Carbohydrate 1.7g, of which sugars 1.6g; Fat 16.9g, of which saturates 2.6g; Cholesterol 72mg; Calcium 68mg; Fibre 1.1g; Sodium 30mg.

MEAT & POULTRY

Red meats dominate in Bulgaria
and Romania, with veal, pork,
beef and lamb often on the menu.
Meat recipes are often linked with
religious festivals – swine are
slaughtered before Christmas
and used for celebration dishes
such as sarmale, and lamb
dishes usually mark the end of
the fasting period of Lent. Meat
can be roasted, wrapped in vine
leaves and baked, grilled as
rissoles or marinated and stored
for the warm summer months.
Mostly, however, it is prepared
with vegetables in hearty, slow-
cooked, full-flavoured stews.

Slow-cooked meats and deep flavours

Whether grilled, roasted, baked, fried, steamed or stewed, every one of the meat recipes shown here will give you a warming meal with tantalizing flavour. All based on traditional dishes, options include Oxtail Stuffed with Mămăligă, a type of polenta; Veal with Grapes and Apricots; the Romanian Goulash with Spätzle, which are small poached dumplings; or Kunka's Moussaka, a Bulgarian recipe with Turkish roots.

Lamb and pork dishes are the everyday choices in Bulgaria. Chicken is now enjoyed as a healthy option, although in the past it was an expensive meat that was used only for special occasions. Veal, with its soft, tender texture and delicate taste is probably the most popular component of Bulgarian meat dishes, but it is more expensive than alternative types of meat.

In Romania, pork and veal are favourites, with beef and lamb following closely. All efforts are made to use every part of the animal so that nothing goes to waste. Meat can be grilled or roasted but will more usually form part of vegetable-based stews. One typical preparation method is to create sausage-like fingers of mititei, tidbits of seasoned meat and offal, grilled over an open fire, typically served with sour cabbage, hot pickles and dark bread. Chicken, duck and game birds are not often used. During the hunting season, wild meats are easily available, such as wild boar and red deer.

Rolled Chicken Schnitzel with Mustard and Sour Cream Sauce

This Bulgarian recipe is also common in other parts of Eastern Europe. Rolls of chicken breasts are stuffed with wild mushrooms and chicken livers and served with a piquant and creamy sauce. The dish can also be prepared with veal or pork. It is considered a great delicacy, and is usually reserved for special occasions.

Serves 4

4 large chicken breast fillets, about
  185g/6½oz each, skin removed
40ml/8 tsp olive oil
115g/4oz chicken livers, trimmed
  and chopped
1 garlic clove, crushed
115g/4oz/1½ cups wild mushrooms,
  chopped
30ml/2 tbsp plain (all-purpose) flour
salt and ground black pepper
steamed cabbage, to serve

For the sauce

30ml/2 tbsp olive oil
1 shallot, finely chopped
10g/¼oz streaky (fatty) bacon,
  finely chopped
5ml/1 tsp Dijon mustard
100ml/3½fl oz/scant ½ cup white wine
100ml/3½fl oz/scant ½ cup sour cream

1 Put the chicken breast fillets between two sheets of clear film (plastic wrap) and beat with a rolling pin to make them thinner. Season well.

2 In a frying pan heat 30ml/2 tbsp of the oil and cook the chicken livers and garlic for 3 minutes, then add the wild mushrooms and stir for another 2 minutes. Leave to cool.

3 Divide the mushroom mixture evenly among the chicken fillets and roll them neatly into parcels. Secure with wooden cocktail sticks (toothpicks) or string. Roll them in flour to coat well.

4 Heat the remaining oil in a heavy pan and gently fry the rolled schnitzels for 8–10 minutes, turning continuously, until they are evenly brown on all sides and cooked through.

5 Meanwhile make the sauce. Put the olive oil in a pan and fry the shallot and bacon until softened.

6 Add the mustard and white wine to the pan. Simmer to reduce by half, then add the sour cream. Season with salt and pepper. Serve the schnitzels with a generous helping of sauce, and a green vegetable such as cabbage.

COOK'S TIP

Wild mushrooms need careful cleaning. They should never be rinsed, as they will absorb a large amount of the water. Instead, using a damp pastry brush, gently brush the surface to clean them.

PER SERVING: Energy 571kcal/2380kJ; Protein 46.2g; Carbohydrate 8.4g, of which sugars 2.1g; Fat 36.6g, of which saturates 9.1g; Cholesterol 201mg; Calcium 62mg; Fibre 0.8g; Sodium 195mg.

Chicken and Thyme Fricassée

This satisfying fricassée, frikase ot pile, originates from Bulgaria. The chicken is cooked on a bed of vegetables, then combined with a light and creamy sauce.

1 Preheat the oven to 160°C/325°F/ Gas 3. Cut the chicken into quarters.

2 Heat the oil in a flameproof casserole over medium heat and cook the onion for 5–10 minutes, or until lightly browned. Add the leeks, carrots and celery, and sauté for 5 minutes.

3 Put the chicken on the vegetables, then pour in the wine and chicken stock. Add the cloves, parsley and bay leaves, season and bring to the boil.

4 Cook the casserole in the oven for 1½ hours. Remove, pour out the liquid and set aside. Keep the casserole warm.

5 In a shallow pan, melt the butter over medium heat, then stir in the flour and cook until light brown. Gradually add most of the reserved cooking liquid, stirring until the sauce is thick and smooth.

6 Put the egg yolks in a bowl and mix in the cream. Stir into the fricassée sauce and simmer gently – do not allow to boil.

7 Add the thyme to the sauce, and pour into the casserole with the chicken. Put the chicken back on the stove and simmer for 2–3 minutes to heat through. Serve with plain rice.

Serves 4
1 chicken, about 1.3kg/3lb in weight
30ml/2 tbsp olive oil
1 onion, chopped
3 leeks, sliced
2 carrots, sliced
2 celery stalks, sliced
100ml/3½fl oz/scant ½ cup dry white wine
300ml/½ pint/1¼ cups chicken stock
10 cloves
2 parsley sprigs
5 fresh bay leaves
45g/1¾oz/3½ tbsp butter
30ml/2 tbsp plain (all-purpose) flour
3 egg yolks
150ml/1¼ pint/⅔ cup single (light) cream
30ml/2 tbsp chopped fresh thyme
salt and ground black pepper

PER SERVING: Energy 773kcal/3208kJ; Protein 47.1g; Carbohydrate 16.2g, of which sugars 8.9g; Fat 56.3g, of which saturates 20.8g; Cholesterol 412mg; Calcium 136mg; Fibre 4.8g; Sodium 280mg.

Serves 4

1 large whole duck, about 1.8kg/4lb
3 thyme sprigs
4–5 parsley sprigs
3 rosemary sprigs
1 carrot, roughly chopped
1 celery stick
1 onion, halved
salt and ground black pepper

For the glaze

400g/14oz apricot compôte
10ml/2 tsp clear honey
15ml/1 tbsp apricot jam
juice of 1 small lemon
juice of 1 small orange

Duck with Apricot and Honey

The summer months bring an abundance of apricots. They are often made into preserves, and used in savoury dishes such as this one, rață cu sos de miere și prune. This uses apricot compôte and jam with honey to make a fragrant glaze, giving a sweet complement to the duck.

1 Preheat the oven to 200°C/400°F/Gas 6. Prepare the duck by washing it well, then drying and seasoning it with salt and pepper.

2 Put the herbs, carrot, celery and onion into the cavity. Put the duck in a roasting pan and, once the oven has reached its correct temperature, roast for 30 minutes.

3 Meanwhile, make the apricot and honey glaze. Pour the syrup from the apricot compôte into a small pan and bring to a gentle boil, then simmer to reduce; this will take about 10 minutes.

4 Finely chop the apricots from the compôte and set aside. Add the honey to the pan, with the apricot jam and the lemon and orange juice, and simmer for 3–5 more minutes. Season to taste with salt and pepper and add the chopped apricots.

5 Remove the duck from the oven, and pour the glaze all over the breast and legs, then return to the oven, and reduce the temperature to 180°C/350°F/Gas 4. Cook for a further 1–1½ hours, basting regularly with the cooking juices and glaze. The duck is ready when the skin is crispy and a deep golden colour.

PER SERVING: Energy 210kcal/885kJ; Protein 25g; Carbohydrate 10g, of which sugars 10g; Fat 8.2g, of which saturates 2.7g; Cholesterol 135mg; Calcium 23mg; Fibre 0.5g; Sodium 145mg.

Serves 4–6
45ml/3 tbsp olive oil
800g/1¾lb beef topside (pot roast), cut
   into 5–6cm/2–2½in cubes
1 onion, finely chopped
3 garlic cloves, crushed
5ml/1 tsp sweet paprika
4 ripe tomatoes, diced
200ml/7fl oz/scant 1 cup red wine
200ml/7fl oz/scant 1 cup
   beef stock
1 bay leaf
5–6 thyme sprigs
800g/1¾lb small pickling (pearl)
   onions, peeled
salt and ground black pepper

Monk's Stew

This Bulgarian meat stew, or gyuvetch, is a version of the Greek dish stifado, and has variations all over the Balkans. The recipe was created by monks from the Rila monastery and was served following periods of fasting. A version of this stew, stufat de miel, is a traditional Easter meal in Romania.

1 Heat the oil in a flameproof casserole over medium heat and add the beef. Cook evenly on all sides, for 5–8 minutes.

2 Remove the beef with a slotted spoon and set aside until needed.

3 Add the onion and garlic to the casserole and sauté for 2 minutes. Add the paprika, tomatoes, red wine and stock.

4 Return the meat to the casserole and add the bay leaf and thyme. Season to taste and cover. Cook over low-medium heat for 1 hour.

5 Add the pickling onions and reduce the heat to low. Cover and continue cooking for a further 45 minutes, by which time the cooking juices will have thickened. Serve with rice or mashed potato and a yogurt salad.

PER SERVING: Energy 383kcal/1595kJ; Protein 33g; Carbohydrate 16.7g, of which sugars 12.4g; Fat 18.5g, of which saturates 5.9g; Cholesterol 77mg; Calcium 60mg; Fibre 3.2g; Sodium 100mg.

Serves 6

350g/12oz/1½ cups minced (ground) pork
200g/7oz/scant 1 cup minced
   (ground) veal
2 medium onions, grated
30ml/2 tbsp ground cumin
1.5ml/¼ tsp ground black pepper
salt

Bulgarian Kebabcheta

Kebabcheta is the best-kept culinary secret in Bulgaria; these juicy chargrilled rissoles are divine. They can be grilled, broiled, pan-fried or baked. Here they are made with a mixture of pork and veal and grilled or barbecued.

1 Put the pork and veal in a large bowl with the onions, cumin, pepper and salt and combine. Cover and rest in the refrigerator for 2 hours.

2 When ready to cook the rissoles, preheat the grill (broiler) or a barbecue to a hot temperature.

3 Add 120ml/4fl oz/½ cup water to the meat mixture and mix to combine.

4 Shape the meat into 7.5cm/ 3in long sausage shapes and cook for 5 minutes on each side, or until the juices run clear. Serve them hot, with a salad.

PER SERVING: Energy 183kcal/763kJ; Protein 18.7g; Carbohydrate 6.9g, of which sugars 4.7g; Fat 9.2g, of which saturates 3.3g; Cholesterol 61mg; Calcium 29mg; Fibre 1.2g; Sodium 63mg.

Serves 4

100ml/3½fl oz/scant ½ cup milk
pinch of freshly grated nutmeg
115g/4oz/2 cups fresh breadcrumbs
1 small onion, finely chopped
½ bunch fresh parsley, leaves
    finely chopped
1 egg, beaten
300g/11oz/scant 1½ cups minced
    (ground) beef
200g/7oz/scant 1 cup minced (ground) veal
45ml/3 tbsp plain (all-purpose) flour
60ml/4 tbsp olive oil
salt and ground black pepper

For the sauce

3 eggs
400g/14oz/1¾ cups thick natural
    (plain) yogurt
45ml/3 tbsp freshly grated
    Parmesan cheese

Meatballs Guvech

Guvech is the Turkish word for baked fish and meat, but the method is also commonly used when preparing fresh vegetables. This meatball version, which is baked in a yogurt sauce, has its roots in Turkish cuisine and is a real favourite in Bulgaria.

1 Preheat the oven to 180°C/350°F/ Gas 4. Pour the milk into a medium bowl and add the nutmeg and breadcrumbs. Leave to soak. Squeeze out the excess liquid and put the breadcrumbs in a large mixing bowl.

2 Add the onion, parsley, egg and minced meats to the soaked breadcrumbs and mix thoroughly. Season with salt and pepper.

3 Shape the mixture into balls. Flatten them slightly and dust with flour.

4 Heat the oil in a large frying pan over medium heat, and sauté the meatballs for about 3–4 minutes on each side. Arrange them in a shallow baking dish.

5 To make the sauce, put the eggs in a bowl and beat them with a little salt and pepper. Gradually add the yogurt and the grated Parmesan cheese. Pour the sauce over the meatballs in the baking dish. Bake for 35–40 minutes, or until golden brown on top.

PER SERVING: Energy 660kcal/2760kJ; Protein 44.2g; Carbohydrate 39.1g, of which sugars 8.6g; Fat 37.8g, of which saturates 12.7g; Cholesterol 284mg; Calcium 409mg; Fibre 1.2g; Sodium 594mg.

Serves 4
1 Savoy cabbage
50ml/2fl oz/¼ cup lemon juice
15ml/1 tbsp clear honey
25ml/1½ tbsp water

For the filling
400g/14oz/1¾ cups minced (ground) veal
1 small bunch parsley, leaves
  finely chopped
115g/4oz/generous ½ cup long grain rice
1 small onion, finely chopped
salt and ground black pepper

Veal-stuffed Cabbage Leaves

Eastern Europeans have many versions of stuffed cabbage leaf recipes. The cabbage used
can be fresh or pickled. This dish uses fresh Savoy cabbage, which often makes an
appearance in the Bulgarian kitchen during the summer, and is lighter than the version
with pickled cabbage. Pork is often used, but veal tastes particularly good.

1 Prepare the cabbage by cutting out
its core with a sharp knife.

2 Put the whole cabbage in a large
pan filled with hot water and simmer
for 15–18 minutes, or until the leaves
are soft. Drain and carefully remove
the leaves. Preheat the oven to
160°C/325°F/Gas 3.

3 To make the filling, mix together
the veal, parsley, rice and onion.
Season well.

4 Spread each cabbage leaf on your
work surface and put a spoonful of
the meat mixture in the centre. Fold
over the top and roll up, tucking in
both sides to make a small parcel.

5 Use wooden cocktail sticks
(toothpicks) to secure the stuffed
cabbage leaves during cooking. Put
them in a single layer, seam side
down, in a wide but deep dish.

6 Add the lemon juice, honey and
water, then cover the dish with foil.
Cook in the oven for 1–1½ hours.
Serve immediately.

PER SERVING: Energy 316kcal/1323kJ; Protein 25.5g; Carbohydrate 36.3g, of which sugars 12g; Fat 7.7g, of which saturates 2.9g; Cholesterol 62mg; Calcium 126mg; Fibre 4.5g; Sodium 99mg.

Oxtail Stuffed with Mămăligă

Polenta was for a long time the mainstay of diets in many south-eastern European countries, mainly because it was a cheap and tastier substitute for traditional grains. It became a staple for the Jews in Romania, where it is known as mămăligă, and here it is enriched with cheese and used to stuff tender rounds of oxtail that have been marinated and cooked in red wine and a variety of flavourings. Although there are a number of stages to this recipe, it is worth the effort. Start preparations the night before.

Serves 4
2 whole oxtails, chopped in segments
20g/¾oz/1½ tbsp butter
1 x 300g/11oz can chopped tomatoes
600ml/1 pint/2½ cups strong
   chicken stock
rind and juice of 1 large orange

For the marinade
800ml/27fl oz/scant 3¼ cups red wine
1 red onion, chopped
1 carrot, chopped
1 celery stick, chopped
2 garlic cloves, crushed
2 thyme sprigs

For the stuffing
300ml/½ pint/1¼ cups milk,
   plus extra if needed
115g/4oz/1 cup polenta
50g/2oz/¼ cup butter
115g/4oz/1 cup grated Cheddar cheese
salt and ground black pepper

1 Mix all the marinade ingredients in a large bowl, then add the oxtail pieces, making sure that they are all covered by the marinade. Cover and chill in the refrigerator overnight.

2 Preheat the oven to 180°C/350°F/Gas 4. Remove the meat and strain the vegetables and herbs, reserving the vegetable mixture and marinade.

3 Heat the butter in a large, heavy non-stick pan that has a lid and briefly brown the oxtail pieces. Add the vegetables and herbs from the marinade. Cover with a lid and continue to brown for 5–8 minutes.

4 Add the tomatoes, chicken stock, and orange rind and juice. Pour in the reserved marinade. Cook in the oven for 2 hours.

5 Prepare the stuffing when the oxtail is almost cooked. Put the milk in a large pan and bring to the boil. Pour in the polenta in a steady stream, stirring constantly to avoid lumps forming. Season to taste. Cook for 15–20 minutes, stirring frequently. The polenta will thicken as it absorbs all the liquid; add more milk if needed. The consistency should be fairly thick. Stir in the butter and cheese. Remove from the heat, and cover.

6 When the oxtail is cooked, remove from the oven and cool slightly. Using a slotted spoon, lift and remove the pieces from the pan and carefully remove the centre bones from each of the oxtail pieces. Discard the bones. Using a small spoon, put some stuffing into the middle of each of the circular oxtail pieces. Serve two to three oxtail pieces per portion.

PER SERVING: Energy 846kcal/3533kJ; Protein 57g; Carbohydrate 27.7g, of which sugars 6.7g; Fat 41.2g, of which saturates 13.8g; Cholesterol 61mg; Calcium 343mg; Fibre 1.4g; Sodium 640mg.

Serves 4

15ml/1 tbsp clear honey
5ml/1 tsp grated fresh root ginger
5ml/1 tsp ground cinnamon
5ml/1 tsp ground black pepper
100ml/3½fl oz/scant ½ cup white wine
800g/1¾lb veal shoulder, cut into
    3cm/1¼in cubes
45ml/3 tbsp olive oil
1 onion, chopped
1 cinnamon stick
30ml/2 tbsp black sesame seeds
115g/4oz seedless grapes, halved
115g/4oz fresh apricots, halved and
    stoned (pitted)

Veal with Grapes and Apricots

This recipe has many versions – this one, of Turkish and Bulgarian origin, is prepared using fresh summer fruits. It can also be made with dried fruits. The veal has to be marinated, so start preparations the day before.

1 In a large bowl combine the honey, ginger, cinnamon, pepper and wine. Rub this mixture over the veal, then cover and let it marinate in the refrigerator overnight.

2 Drain the veal and set the marinade aside. Heat the olive oil in a large sauté pan, and sauté the onion until just golden in colour, then add the veal cubes and brown evenly.

3 Add the reserved marinade, 300ml/½ pint/1¼ cups water and the cinnamon stick, and simmer for 30 minutes, or until the liquid has reduced by about half, and the veal is cooked.

4 Meanwhile, put the sesame seeds in a dry pan and toast over medium-high heat, tossing regularly, for 1 minute.

5 Add the grapes and apricot halves and simmer in the pan for a further 5–8 minutes. Serve immediately, sprinkled with the sesame seeds, and accompanied by plain rice.

PER SERVING: Energy 405kcal/1696kJ; Protein 44.7g; Carbohydrate 11.3g, of which sugars 9.6g; Fat 18.7g, of which saturates 3.7g; Cholesterol 168mg; Calcium 86mg; Fibre 1.3g; Sodium 226mg.

Serves 6

1kg/2¼lb sauerkraut
60ml/4 tbsp olive oil
2 small onions, chopped
800g/1¾lb pork fillet (tenderloin), cut into
  2cm/¾in cubes
5ml/1 tsp salt
7.5ml/1½ tsp paprika
1 large tomato, chopped
5ml/1 tsp caraway seeds
60ml/4 tbsp buttermilk
120ml/4fl oz/½ cup sour cream

For the spätzle

250g/9oz/2¼ cups plain
  (all-purpose) flour
2.5ml/½ tsp salt
1.5ml/¼ tsp ground black pepper
1.5ml/¼ tsp freshly grated nutmeg
2 eggs
30ml/2 tbsp double (heavy) cream

Goulash with Spätzle

This goulash, gulaş cu perişoare, originates from the wilds of Transylvania, where there are still strong Hungarian and Germanic culinary influences. Spätzle are small dumplings that are poached and then served with the goulash.

1 Squeeze the liquid out of the sauerkraut. Put the oil into a flameproof casserole or large, heavy pan and sauté the onions until soft. Remove the onions using a slotted spoon and set side. Add the pork to the casserole and brown all over.

2 Return the onions to the casserole, with the salt, paprika, chopped tomato and caraway seeds. Stir well and put the sauerkraut on top.

3 Pour in enough water to just cover the sauerkraut, and cover with a lid. Simmer gently for at least 25 minutes, or until the meat and cabbage are tender. Add more water if needed.

4 To make the spätzle, put the flour in a bowl with the salt, pepper and nutmeg. Stir in the eggs and cream to make a dough. Have a large pan of salted boiling water ready.

5 Using your hands, shape the dough into small dumplings. Ten minutes before the meat is ready, drop the dumplings a few at a time into the water. They are cooked when they rise to the top. Remove with a slotted spoon and keep warm.

6 When the meat is ready, stir in the buttermilk and sour cream. Season to taste and simmer for a few more minutes. Serve the goulash with the spätzle.

PER SERVING: Energy 501kcal/2095kJ; Protein 38.2g; Carbohydrate 40.6g, of which sugars 7.7g; Fat 22g, of which saturates 7.5g; Cholesterol 166mg; Calcium 209mg; Fibre 6g; Sodium 1449mg.

Serves 4

2 pork fillets (tenderloins), about
   400g/14oz each
45ml/3 tbsp vegetable oil
1 onion, chopped
5ml/1 tsp sweet paprika, plus extra to
   garnish
2 green (bell) peppers, thinly sliced
   into rings
1 tomato, chopped
300ml/½ pint/1¼ cups sour cream,
   plus extra to serve
salt and ground black pepper

Bulgarian-style Paprikash

Paprikash, generally thought of as a Hungarian dish, is a thick, paprika-based stew, made with veal, chicken or rabbit. Red meat is not a traditional component, although pork is used here and beef and lamb also work well.

1 Dice the pork into 3cm/1¼in cubes. Heat the oil in a flameproof casserole over medium heat and cook the onion for 5–10 minutes, or until a golden colour.

2 Remove the casserole from the heat and stir in the paprika, then add 100ml/3½fl oz/scant ½ cup water.

3 Return the casserole to the heat and simmer for 2–3 minutes.

4 Add the meat to the casserole and season well. Cover and simmer for 30–40 minutes.

5 By now the sauce should have thickened to a syrupy consistency. Add the sliced peppers and tomato, and cook for a further 5–6 minutes.

6 Stir in the sour cream and heat through. Serve with plain boiled rice and a dollop of sour cream.

PER SERVING: Energy 535kcal/2226kJ; Protein 47.1g; Carbohydrate 15.6g, of which sugars 13.2g; Fat 31.9g, of which saturates 13.2g; Cholesterol 171mg; Calcium 114mg; Fibre 2.7g; Sodium 179mg.

Serves 4

400g/14oz/1¾ cups minced (ground) pork
1 onion, chopped
65g/2½oz short grain rice
30ml/2 tbsp vegetable oil
10ml/2 tsp dried thyme
60ml/4 tbsp chopped fresh dill
20 sauerkraut leaves about 5cm/2in x
    5cm/2in, fewer leaves if they are larger
salt and ground black pepper

Romanian Stuffed Sauerkraut

Bulgarians and Romanians have a soft spot for sauerkraut, and here the whole leaves of this popular pickled cabbage are stuffed with pork, rice and herbs. In Romania this dish is known as sarmale în foi de varză, and is often made in small shapes and eaten as finger food. Although some recipes can take a long time to prepare, this version is an easier one.

1 Put the pork in a large bowl and mix with the onion, rice, oil, thyme and dill. Season with salt and pepper.

2 Remove the central rib of each of the sauerkraut leaves. Spoon a rounded spoonful of stuffing on to each leaf and fold over the ends, then roll into a small sausage shape.

3 Arrange the stuffed leaves in a pan, tightly fitting them against one another. Cover with boiling water from the kettle.

4 Weigh the rolls down with a plate and put the pan on the heat to simmer for 30–45 minutes. Serve.

COOK'S TIPS

• A good accompaniment for the sarmale is a light tomato sauce or a mushroom and cream sauce.

• Bags of fresh sauerkraut are usually found in the chilled or delicatessen sections of supermarkets. The sauerkraut should be washed before use.

PER SERVING: Energy 309kcal/1286kJ; Protein 22.4g; Carbohydrate 19.5g, of which sugars 6g; Fat 15.7g, of which saturates 4.2g; Cholesterol 66mg; Calcium 88mg; Fibre 2.9g; Sodium 78mg.

Vine Leaves Stuffed with Pork, Pine Nuts and Raisins

This recipe for stuffed vine leaves is equally popular in both Bulgaria and Romania, and although it would normally be made with fresh vine leaves, packets of preserved leaves are quite acceptable. Serve with yogurt, preferably Bulgarian.

Serves 4

300g/11oz packet vine leaves, or
    40 fresh vine leaves
30ml/2 tbsp olive oil
1 medium shallot, finely chopped
400g/14oz/1¾ cups finely minced
    (ground) pork
150g/5oz/scant ¾ cup long grain rice
100ml/3½fl oz/scant ½ cup chicken stock
2.5ml/½ tsp ground cumin
80g/3¼oz/¾ cup pine nuts, chopped
80g/3¼oz/⅔ cup raisins
1 small bunch parsley,
    leaves finely chopped
30ml/2 tbsp chopped fresh mint
salt and ground black pepper

1 If using fresh vine leaves, put the leaves in a bowl and cover with hot water. Stand for 5 minutes, then drain. If you are using leaves in brine, put them into a bowl and cover with cold water to soak for 15 minutes, then drain. Set aside.

2 Heat the olive oil in a deep frying pan over medium heat, add the shallot and cook for 5 minutes, or until soft. Add the pork to the shallot and cook, stirring constantly, until the meat is browned.

3 Add the rice and chicken stock to the mince and simmer for about 10 minutes. Stir in the cumin and season to taste. When most of the liquid has been absorbed, add the pine nuts and raisins.

4 Remove from the heat, cover with a clean dish towel and lid, then leave to stand for 10 minutes. Add the parsley and mint, and mix well.

5 Line a large, heavy pan with about five of the vine leaves (use torn or broken leaves for this, keeping the best leaves for stuffing). Set aside three to five leaves to use to cover the top. Lay one of the remaining leaves on the work surface, with the stalk towards you, and put a heaped teaspoon of the pork mixture just above the stalk and just below the centre of the leaf. Wrap the vine leaf by folding in from the stalk end, then fold both sides of the leaf into the centre and roll the leaf up to make a cylinder. Continue until all the stuffing and leaves are used up.

6 Put each stuffed leaf in the lined pan, join side down, packing them tightly with about 15–20 in each layer. You should have two layers. Add enough water to cover three-quarters of the way up the stuffed leaves. Cover with the reserved loose leaves and weigh down with a plate. Simmer over low heat for 45 minutes, then remove from the heat and allow to cool.

PER SERVING: Energy 565kcal/2354kJ; Protein 26.6g; Carbohydrate 48.7g, of which sugars 18.6g; Fat 29.5g, of which saturates 5.3g; Cholesterol 66mg; Calcium 87mg; Fibre 3g; Sodium 88mg.

Serves 6

100ml/3½fl oz/scant ½ cup milk

2 slices of white bread

5 large (US extra large) eggs

1 large onion, grated

350g/12oz/1½ cups minced
   (ground) beef

350g/12oz/1½ cups minced
   (ground) pork

leaves from 1 small bunch
   fresh thyme

½ small bunch of parsley leaves,
   chopped

12 smoked streaky (fatty) bacon
   rashers (strips)

salt and ground black pepper

Meat Loaf

The Eastern European answer to fast food is a meat loaf, prepared using a mixture of good-quality veal or beef and pork. This Transylvanian recipe, cozonac de carne, uses smoked ham or bacon to wrap the loaf.

1 Preheat the oven to 180°C/350°F/Gas 4 and grease a 20–25cm/8–10in loaf tin. Put the milk in a bowl and add the bread slices. Leave to soak for a few minutes then squeeze out the excess liquid.

2 Bring a small pan of water to the boil and cook four eggs for 7 minutes. Remove and leave to cool completely.

3 Put the soaked bread in a large bowl, add the onion, beef, pork, thyme and parsley. Beat the remaining egg and add to the bowl. Season with salt and pepper. Combine the mixture well.

4 Line the loaf tin with bacon rashers, leaving enough hanging over the edges for wrapping around the loaf.

5 Fill the tin with the meat mixture. Peel the eggs and gently press into the loaf, along its full length, burying the eggs into the centre.

6 Wrap the bacon rashers around the meat loaf. Place the tin on a baking tray. Bake for 1 hour, or until the loaf is golden brown. Serve hot or cold.

PER SERVING: Energy 401kcal/1673kJ; Protein 33.1g; Carbohydrate 11.3g, of which sugars 5g; Fat 25.4g, of which saturates 9.3g; Cholesterol 250mg; Calcium 102mg; Fibre 1.5g; Sodium 476mg.

Serves 4

450g/1lb lamb fillet or neck of lamb,
cut into 2–3cm/¾–1¼in cubes

2 red onions or shallots, peeled

200g/7oz smoked pancetta, cut into
2–3cm/¾–1¼in cubes

16 cherry tomatoes

2 green (bell) peppers, seeded and
cut into pieces

45ml/3 tbsp olive oil, for brushing

salt and ground black pepper

For the marinade

150ml/¼ pt/⅔ cup olive oil

juice of 1 lemon

1 garlic clove, crushed

mixed herbs

Lamb Shish Kebab

Romanian shish kebab, frigarui e oaie la gratăr, is made either with pork and beef, or lamb, which is a more traditional option. This version uses tender lamb fillet or neck of lamb combined with pancetta and vegetables.

1 Blend all the marinade ingredients in a bowl. Put the lamb into a shallow dish and pour the marinade over the meat. Cover and leave in the refrigerator overnight.

2 Quarter the onions or shallots. Have eight long skewers ready and preheat the grill (broiler) or barbecue to high. When ready to cook, thread the cubes of lamb on to the skewers, alternating them with the pancetta cubes, cherry tomatoes, onion quarters and peppers.

3 Brush the prepared kebabs with the olive oil and season with salt and pepper.

4 Cook the kebabs, turning to brown on all sides, for 6–8 minutes, or until cooked through. Serve with a salad.

COOK'S TIP

Marinating the lamb cubes overnight adds flavour and tenderizes the meat; this is not essential, but the kebabs taste much better for it.

PER SERVING: Energy 361kcal/1515kJ; Protein 22.5g; Carbohydrate 38.4g, of which sugars 8.1g; Fat 14.1g, of which saturates 5.1g; Cholesterol 64mg; Calcium 133mg; Fibre 3g; Sodium 249mg.

Serves 4

150g/5oz lamb sweetbreads, washed
200g/7oz leg of lamb, cut into
2–3cm/¾–1¼in pieces
4 small lamb cutlets (US rib chops)
weighing 125g/4¼oz, trimmed
2 lamb's kidneys, halved
150g/5oz lamb's liver, cut into pieces
75ml/5 tbsp olive oil
5ml/1 tsp green peppercorns, crushed
1 small bunch rosemary, leaves chopped
salt

Mixed Lamb Kebab

This, called meshena agneshska skara, is the most delicious of Bulgarian kebabs. It is best made with tender and sweet spring lamb, using leg meat, lamb cutlets, sweetbreads, kidney and liver.

1 Put the sweetbreads into simmering water for 3 minutes to blanch them. Drain immediately and run under cold water to stop the cooking process. Once cool, remove the membrane, or vein, and divide into pieces.

2 Put all the lamb pieces, the leg, cutlets, sweetbreads, kidneys and liver in a large, shallow dish and drizzle with the olive oil.

3 Sprinkle with the green peppercorns and rosemary and season with some salt. Cover and allow to rest in the refrigerator for 2 hours.

4 Have four long skewers ready and preheat a grill (broiler) or barbecue. Skewer the meats on to the skewers. Grill (broil) or barbecue on high for 8–10 minutes or until cooked. Serve with a salad and plain rice.

PER SERVING: Energy 408kcal/1697kJ; Protein 33.3g; Carbohydrate 0.6g, of which sugars 0g; Fat 28.8g, of which saturates 8.6g; Cholesterol 421mg; Calcium 15mg; Fibre 0g; Sodium 182mg.

Shoulder of Lamb Yahnia with Spring Onion

Serves 4

45ml/3 tbsp extra virgin olive oil
500g/1¼lb shoulder of lamb, off the bone, cut into 2–4cm/¾–1½in cubes
1 ripe tomato, finely chopped
2.5ml/½ tsp ground cumin
200ml/7fl oz/scant 1 cup lamb stock
6 bunches of spring onions (scallions), trimmed and chopped
100ml/3½fl oz/scant ½ cup thick natural (plain) yogurt, to serve
salt and ground black pepper

Yahnia dishes are light stews – this one has Turkish overtones and is a typical spring favourite in Bulgaria. The large quantity of spring onions in this dish bring a mild and delicate flavour to the lamb.

1 Heat the olive oil in a flameproof casserole or large, heavy pan, add the lamb cubes and sauté for 6–8 minutes over medium heat.

2 Season the casserole mixture with salt and pepper. Add the tomato and cumin. Stir well and pour in the stock.

3 Bring to the boil, then cover the casserole or pan and simmer for 1 hour, or until the lamb is tender and the cooking liquid reduced.

4 Add the spring onions and stir in well. Simmer for a further 15 minutes. Serve hot with a dollop of yogurt and a portion of rice.

Bulgarian Braised Lamb with Prunes

The warm flavours of bay leaves, cinnamon and cloves go very well with the sweetness of prunes in this dish of tender leg of lamb. Serve with rice or boiled potatoes.

1 Heat the oil in a flameproof casserole, add the onion and sauté until lightly coloured.

2 Put the flour on a plate and season with salt and pepper. Add the meat and dust all over. Put the meat in the casserole and cook until browned on all sides.

3 Add the stock and simmer for 20–30 minutes, or until the sauce has slightly thickened.

4 Add the sugar, vinegar, bay leaves, cinnamon, cloves and prunes to the casserole. Bring to a boil, and simmer for a further 20 minutes, or until the meat is tender. Serve hot.

Serves 4

75ml/5 tbsp vegetable oil
1 large onion, finely chopped
30ml/2 tbsp plain (all-purpose) flour
600g/1lb 5oz boned leg of lamb, cut into 5cm/2in cubes
200ml/7fl oz/scant 1 cup stock made from the lamb bones
15ml/1 tbsp caster (superfine) sugar
75ml/5 tbsp white wine vinegar
2 bay leaves
2.5ml/½ tsp ground cinnamon
pinch of ground cloves
200g/7oz/scant 1 cup ready-to-eat prunes
salt and ground black pepper

PER SERVING: Energy 530kcal/2215kJ; Protein 32.3g; Carbohydrate 32.7g, of which sugars 25.2g; Fat 31g, of which saturates 9.3g; Cholesterol 114mg; Calcium 60mg; Fibre 4.1g; Sodium 137mg.

Serves 4

800g/1¾lb/3½ cups finely minced (ground) lamb

1 large onion, grated

15ml/1 tbsp salt

2 large (US extra large) eggs

1 small bunch coriander (cilantro) leaves, chopped

10ml/2 tsp ground cumin

5ml/1 tsp chopped fresh thyme

5ml/1 tsp ground allspice

30ml/2 tbsp vegetable oil

Lamb Kofta

A term based on a Persian word, kofta are common to Bulgaria (where they are kyufte) and Romania (where they are chiftele). A perfect dish for grilling or griddling, these meatballs are made entirely with lamb.

1 Put the lamb in a food processor and add the onion and salt. Process until it forms a paste and transfer to a large bowl.

2 Add the eggs, coriander, cumin, thyme and allspice. Wet your hands with a little water and combine well.

3 Shape the meat into evenly sized small sausages.

4 Cook the kofta under a hot grill (broiler), or on a preheated griddle, for about 8 minutes on each side, or until cooked through and golden. Serve with a salad.

PER SERVING: Energy 526kcal/2188kJ; Protein 43.3g; Carbohydrate 9.1g, of which sugars 5.9g; Fat 35.6g, of which saturates 13.8g; Cholesterol 249mg; Calcium 103mg; Fibre 2g; Sodium 672mg.

Kunka's Moussaka

Many Bulgarians have Turkish antecedents, and recipes such as this one, from the author's Bulgarian mother, are often passed down through the generations. Most moussakas include potatoes and sometimes courgettes, but this aubergine version is rich and flavoursome.

Serves 6

30ml/2 tbsp olive oil, plus extra for frying and greasing
2 large aubergines (eggplants)
1 large onion, finely chopped
4 garlic cloves, crushed
400g/14oz/1¾ cups minced (ground) lamb
400g/14oz can plum tomatoes
15ml/1 tbsp finely chopped fresh oregano
30ml/2 tbsp finely chopped fresh parsley
2 large beefsteak or plum tomatoes
salt and ground black pepper

1 Grease a 25 x 10 x 4cm/10 x 4 x 1½in baking dish lightly with oil. Slice the aubergines lengthways into 5mm/¼in thick slices.

2 In a large non-stick pan, heat some olive oil and fry the aubergine slices a few at a time, turning them over and making sure that they are evenly browned and cooked. Using a slotted spatula, transfer the aubergine slices to kitchen paper to drain off the excess fat. Sprinkle with salt. Repeat until you have cooked all the aubergine, adding more oil to the pan if necessary. Set the aubergine aside.

3 Heat 30ml/2 tbsp oil in a large, heavy pan, and sauté the onion and garlic for 5 minutes, or until softened. Add the lamb and cook, stirring, for about 10 minutes, or until the meat is browned.

4 Add the canned tomatoes and simmer for a further 10 minutes. Season to taste and add the oregano and parsley.

5 Preheat the oven to 180°C/350°F/Gas 4. Slice the large beefsteak or plum tomatoes horizontally into 5mm/¼in slices and set aside.

6 To assemble the moussaka, line the base of the dish with one-third of the aubergine slices, overlapping them slightly. Cover with half the lamb mixture, then cover with half the remaining aubergine slices. Add the second half of the meat mixture. Cover with the remaining aubergine slices and arrange the tomato slices over the top.

7 Bake for 40 minutes and serve warm with a side salad of tomatoes, cucumber and onion.

COOK'S TIP

When aubergine is fried, it absorbs large amounts of oil. You therefore need to work quickly, while making sure that the aubergine is fully cooked, otherwise it will taste bitter.

PER SERVING: Energy 223kcal/930kJ; Protein 15.4g; Carbohydrate 10.7g, of which sugars 9.3g; Fat 13.5g, of which saturates 4.9g; Cholesterol 51mg; Calcium 59mg; Fibre 4.3g; Sodium 66mg.

DESSERTS &
BAKING

With such an abundant fruit
harvest, fresh fruit, fruit compôte
and poached or baked fruit are
all popular choices at the end of
a meal. Other prepared sweets
include the syrup-soaked
textures of Baklava and other
Middle Eastern-style pastries,
sticky strudels, chocolate or fruit-
filled crêpes and rice puddings.
Another option is the tempting
fruit-packed, nutty flavours of
home-baked cakes, often served
with lashings of cream and thick,
sweet Turkish-style coffee.

Butter cream and baklava

Bulgarians and Romanians are fond of cakes and desserts, and take a particular delight in very sweet options, with dishes often drenched in Middle Eastern-style sweet sugar syrups.

The influence of the Ottoman kitchen is clear. Baklava is commonly served in cafés and cake shops in both countries, and although it can be a little time-consuming to prepare, a home-made version is a sublime treat. A luscious dessert platter of juicy peaches, apricots, sweet melons and watermelons also has Ottoman roots, and provides a refreshing, healthy option to conclude a meal. There are many varieties of eating grapes grown and enjoyed throughout Bulgaria and Romania which often feature in sweet dishes. Other fruits include pears, apples, plums, cherries, quinces and various berries, which can be eaten fresh, combined in a purée, baked or poached in dishes such as Baked Quinces in Syrup, or used as sweet fillings for pastries such as Cherry Strudel.

Cakes tend to be rich, covered in butter creams rather than double cream. There is a dazzling array of rich tortes, cakes, filled cakes, strudels with fruits, nuts and poppy seeds, as well as chocolate treats, such as Coffee and Chocolate Cakes and the sweet loaf Romanian Babka.

Serves 4

6 quinces

juice of 2 lemons

200g/7oz/1 cup caster (superfine) sugar

1 vanilla pod (bean), split lengthways

300ml/½ pint/1¼ cups water

4 cloves

200ml/7fl oz/scant 1 cup yogurt, to serve

Baked Quinces in Syrup

Quinces are a favourite all over Bulgaria: fresh in season, preserved in winter. In this recipe they are cooked in quince syrup for a more intense flavour. If you are unable to get hold of quinces, pears can be used instead.

1 Peel four of the quinces and cut into quarters. Remove the cores and put the quince flesh into a large ovenproof dish or casserole with a lid, arranged in a single layer. Pour over the lemon juice.

2 Use the remaining two quinces to make the syrup. Peel, core and chop them coarsely. Put them in a large pan with 115g/4oz/generous ½ cup of the sugar. Scrape out the vanilla seeds and add them to the pan with the pod.

3 Add enough water to cover. Bring to the boil and simmer for 1 hour, or until the quinces are soft and dark red, and the liquid has turned syrupy.

4 Strain the syrup and discard the quince pulp and vanilla pod.

5 Preheat the oven to 120°C/250°F/ Gas ½. Pour the syrup over the quince quarters, making sure they are covered.

6 Add the cloves and remaining sugar. Put a piece of baking parchment on top to keep the fruit submerged.

7 Put on the lid and cook in the oven for 1 hour, or until the quinces are soft to the touch and red in colour. To serve, put four quince quarters with some syrup in each dessert bowl, and add a dollop of yogurt.

PER SERVING: Energy 307kcal/1305kJ; Protein 1.1g; Carbohydrate 79.8g, of which sugars 79.8g; Fat 0.3g, of which saturates 0g; Cholesterol 0mg; Calcium 57mg; Fibre 6.1g; Sodium 11mg.

Serves 6
600g/1lb 5oz apricots, halved
30ml/2 tbsp caster (superfine) sugar
25ml/1½ tbsp ground cinnamon
30ml/2 tbsp honey
45ml/3 tbsp flaked (sliced) almonds
icing (confectioners') sugar, to dust
200ml/7fl oz/scant 1 cup thick natural
   (plain) yogurt, to serve

Baked Sweet Apricots

The hot summers in Bulgaria and Romania bring abundant fruits, sweet, juicy and full of flavour. The plums, apricots, peaches and melons are particularly good. As well as being used fresh while in season, they are preserved for the cold winter months. This simple recipe can be made with any of the fruits mentioned above.

1 Tightly arrange the apricot halves, cut side up, in a shallow roasting pan.

2 Sprinkle with the sugar and cinnamon, then drizzle with the honey. Cover the roasting pan with foil or a dish towel and allow to rest for 2 hours in the refrigerator.

3 Meanwhile, put the almonds in a dry pan and toast over medium-high heat, tossing regularly, for 1–2 minutes, or until golden brown. Set aside.

4 Preheat the oven to 180°C/350°F/Gas 4. Remove the dish towel from the roasting pan. Add 120ml/4fl oz/½ cup water and roast for 30 minutes, or until the contents are soft and golden brown.

5 Sprinkle with the toasted almonds and dust with icing sugar. Serve the apricots in individual bowls with a portion of yogurt.

PER SERVING: Energy 111kcal/470kJ; Protein 2.5g; Carbohydrate 16.8g, of which sugars 16.6g; Fat 4.3g, of which saturates 0.4g; Cholesterol 0mg; Calcium 36mg; Fibre 2.3g; Sodium 4mg.

Baklava

Because of the Ottoman influence, it is no surprise that baklava has the same prominence in Bulgaria as it has in Turkey. This version is made with walnuts, but pistachio nuts are also popular. A touch of rose water adds a delicate fragrance to the syrup.

Serves 12

400g/14oz/scant 2 cups clarified butter, or ordinary butter, melted
500g/1¼lb/3⅓ cups walnuts, roughly chopped
200g/7oz/1 cup caster (superfine) sugar
150g/5oz/1¼ cups ground almonds
25 sheets filo pastry (about 2 packets), thawed if frozen

For the syrup

500g/1¼lb/2¾ cups caster (superfine) sugar
75ml/5 tbsp rose water
juice and finely grated rind of 2 lemons

1 Preheat the oven to 180°C/350°F/Gas 4. Brush a large roasting pan, about 30 x 20cm/12 x 8in, with a little of the clarified butter. Set aside.

2 In a large bowl combine the walnuts and caster sugar. Put the ground almonds in a separate bowl and stir in all but 30ml/2 tbsp of clarified butter.

3 Lay a sheet of filo pastry in the roasting pan. (Cover the remaining filo pastry with a damp dish towel to prevent it from drying out.) Sprinkle with 30ml/2 tbsp of the almond and butter mixture. Cover with another sheet of filo pastry and sprinkle over another 30ml/2 tbsp of the almond mixture. Continue until you have eight layers of filo pastry.

4 Using about half the walnut mixture, spread a layer over the top layer of filo. Cover with eight more layers of filo and ground almonds, alternating as before. Follow with the remainder of the walnut mixture and press down gently.

5 Finish off with eight more filo sheets layered with the ground almond and butter mixture. Butter the top layer with the reserved clarified butter. Using a sharp knife, cut the baklava into small diamond shapes.

6 Spray the baklava or splash lightly with water and bake for 30 minutes. Reduce the oven temperature to 140°C/275°F/Gas 1 and cook the baklava for another 2 hours. Remove from the oven and leave to cool in the tin.

7 To make the syrup, put the sugar and 500ml/17fl oz/generous 2 cups water in a pan and bring to the boil. Reduce the heat to a simmer, add the rose water and cook for about 15 minutes, or until the syrup is thick. Stir in the lemon juice and rind.

8 When the baklava is completely cool, spoon over the hot syrup, making sure that it covers all the pastry. Cover loosely with a clean dish towel, put in a dry place and allow the baklava to settle for 48 hours before serving.

PER SERVING: Energy 839kcal/3490kJ; Protein 9.2g; Carbohydrate 63.2g, of which sugars 62.6g; Fat 62.8g, of which saturates 20.9g; Cholesterol 77mg; Calcium 105mg; Fibre 2.4g; Sodium 258mg.

Serves 6

150g/5oz/⅔ cup mascarpone
115g/4oz/½ cup cream cheese
115g/4oz/generous ½ cup caster
   (superfine) sugar
seeds of 1 vanilla pod (bean)
250ml/8fl oz/1 cup double (heavy) cream
130g/4½oz/generous ½ cup Greek
   (US strained plain) yogurt

For the poached quinces

300g/11oz/1½ cups caster
   (superfine) sugar
1 star anise
2 cinnamon sticks
2 cloves
½ lemon, thickly sliced
2 large quinces

Vanilla Creams with Quince

Quinces are popular in both Romania and Bulgaria and are generally poached or baked. This recipe is a light cream ideal for serving with poached quinces.

1 Put the mascarpone, cream cheese, sugar and vanilla seeds in a mixing bowl and beat until smooth. Add the cream and yogurt, then beat again until thoroughly blended.

2 Line six ramekins with squares of wet muslin (cheesecloth) and spoon in the cream mixture. Put the moulds on a shallow tray, cover with clear film (plastic wrap) and chill to set for at least 8 hours or overnight.

3 Preheat the oven to 150°C/300°F/ Gas 2. Put the sugar, spices and lemon in a flameproof casserole with 1 litre/1¾ pints/4 cups water and bring to the boil. Reduce the heat to a simmer.

4 Peel and core the quinces and cut the flesh into cubes, then add them to the simmering syrup. Cover carefully with a circle of baking parchment to help keep the fruit submerged in the syrup.

5 Cover the casserole with the lid and transfer to the oven to poach for 3–4 hours, until soft and tender. Leave to cool, then chill until needed.

6 Lift the creams out of their moulds using the sides of the muslin to help you. Invert each one on to a serving plate. Spoon some poached quince and syrup around the creams and serve.

PER SERVING: Energy 640kcal/2681kJ; Protein 5.5g; Carbohydrate 81.3g, of which sugars 81.3g; Fat 37.4g, of which saturates 21.6g; Cholesterol 83mg; Calcium 116mg; Fibre 1.5g; Sodium 95mg.

Fruit and Honey Pancakes

These fluffy pancakes, called katmi, are traditionally cooked on a hot griddle and come from the Bulgarian city of Plovdiv. The batter uses yeast to make them extra light.

1 Put the flour in a large bowl and make a well in the centre. Add the warm milk, sugar and salt, and combine. Stir in the egg yolks and add the yeast. Mix well until you have a smooth batter. Cover and leave in a warm place for 1 hour, or until the batter has doubled in size.

2 Put the egg whites into a clean, grease-free bowl and whisk until they form soft peaks. Fold them into the pancake batter. Stir in the sour cream.

3 Put a heavy, non-stick frying pan, about 18cm/7in in diameter, on medium-high heat. Brush its surface with a little clarified butter.

4 Pour a ladleful of the pancake mixture into the pan and cook for about 40 seconds, or until golden brown on the underside and the top is set. Flip over and cook the other side until golden. Serve hot with a drizzle of honey and some berries, dusted with icing sugar.

Makes 12/Serves 6
165g/5½oz/generous 1¼ cups plain (all-purpose) flour
150ml/¼ pint/⅔ cup warm milk
10ml/2 tsp sugar
5ml/1 tsp salt
2 eggs, separated
10g/¼oz fresh yeast, crumbled
15ml/1 tbsp sour cream
10ml/2 tsp clarified butter

For the topping
60ml/4 tbsp clear honey
115g/4oz/1 cup fresh berries, such as raspberries, blueberries or strawberries
icing (confectioners') sugar, for dusting

PER SERVING: Energy 85kcal/361kJ; Protein 2.9g; Carbohydrate 16g, of which sugars 5.5g; Fat 1.6g, of which saturates 0.6g; Cholesterol 33mg; Calcium 42mg; Fibre 0.5g; Sodium 21mg.

Cherry Strudel

Apple is the most common filling for a strudel, but sweet cherries in season mingled with pecan nuts make this fine, crisp and light dessert a real luxury.

Serves 6

65g/2½oz/5 tbsp butter, melted,
    plus extra for greasing
30ml/2 tbsp cherry jam
500g/1¼lb fresh cherries, stoned (pitted)
75g/3oz/½ cup pecan nuts,
    roughly chopped
80g/3¼oz/scant ½ cup caster (superfine)
    sugar, plus extra for sprinkling
25g/1oz/½ cup brioche breadcrumbs
10 large sheets filo pastry,
    thawed if frozen
icing (confectioners') sugar, to decorate

1 Preheat the oven to 200°C/400°F/ Gas 6. Butter and line a baking sheet with baking parchment. Put the cherry jam in a small pan and heat slowly until just melted.

2 In a large bowl combine the cherries, pecan nuts, sugar and brioche breadcrumbs.

3 Lay a damp dish towel on your work surface, then take a sheet of filo pastry and lay on top. (Cover the remaining filo pastry with a damp dish towel to prevent it from drying out.) Brush generously with melted butter, then cover with another sheet of filo and

brush that with butter. Add a third sheet, and brush with the melted cherry jam as well as the butter. Continue in this way, with the third sheet brushed with jam and butter, until all the filo is used up.

4 Put the cherry and pecan mixture down the centre of the pastry and roll the pastry up.

5 Butter the strudel on all sides, sprinkle on some caster sugar and curl into a horseshoe. Put on the baking sheet and bake for 20–30 minutes, or until golden brown. Serve warm or cold, dusted with icing sugar.

PER SERVING: Energy 349kcal/1472kJ; Protein 5.9g; Carbohydrate 59.4g, of which sugars 27.7g; Fat 11.4g, of which saturates 6.3g; Cholesterol 57mg; Calcium 83mg; Fibre 2g; Sodium 128mg.

Serves 6

10 large ready-to-eat prunes, stones
    removed, roughly chopped
30ml/2 tbsp plum brandy
200g/7oz/1 cup pudding rice
400ml/14fl oz/1⅔ cups double
    (heavy) cream
700ml/25fl oz/2¾ cups full-fat
    (whole) milk
150g/5oz/¾ cup caster (superfine) sugar
75ml/5 tbsp orange flower water

Prune Rice Pudding

Rice pudding is often made in the homes of Bulgarian and Romanian families, and each
household will have its own way of preparing it. Pudding rice is used widely in Bulgaria,
not only for making sweet dishes but for savoury as well.

1 Put the prunes in a shallow dish,
cover with the brandy and leave to
soak for at least 1 hour.

2 Combine the rice and two-thirds of
the cream in a heavy pan. Cook over
medium heat for 2–3 minutes. Stir,
then add the milk and all but 30ml/
2 tbsp of the sugar.

3 Cook the mixture over a low
heat, stirring occasionally, for
another 10–15 minutes, or until
the rice grains are soft and the
liquid has been almost totally
absorbed into the rice.

4 Add the remaining double cream
and the orange flower water and
set aside. Preheat the oven to
180°C/350°F/Gas 4.

5 Divide the prunes and the
soaking liquid among six small
ovenproof dishes and cover with
the rice pudding.

6 Bake for 8–10 minutes, or until
the tops are golden. Remove from the
oven and set aside to cool briefly.
Serve while still warm.

PER SERVING: Energy 640kcal/2668kJ; Protein 8.1g; Carbohydrate 68.6g, of which sugars 42g; Fat 40.6g, of which saturates 22.8g; Cholesterol 103mg; Calcium 196mg; Fibre 1.4g; Sodium 93mg.

Makes 12

175g/6oz/1½ cups self-raising
 (self-rising) flour
175g/6oz/¾ cup butter
175g/6oz/scant 1 cup caster
 (superfine) sugar
3 large (US extra large) eggs
45ml/3 tbsp espresso coffee
75g/3oz/½ cup walnuts,
 roughly chopped

For the syrup

50g/2oz/¼ cup light muscovado
 (brown) sugar
30ml/2 tbsp hot espresso coffee

For the topping

50g/2oz milk chocolate
115g/4oz/½ cup mascarpone, at room
 temperature
12 walnut halves, to decorate

Coffee and Chocolate Cakes

Prajitură cu cremă de cafea şi ciocolată is a sweet dish
that you will find in the trendy restaurants in the
centre of Bucharest. These moist cakes are made with
walnuts and topped with chocolate and mascarpone.

1 Preheat the oven to 180°C/350°F/
Gas 4. Put 12 paper cake cases into a
bun or muffin tin (pan). Put the flour
into a large bowl and add the butter,
sugar and eggs. Whisk together until
smooth and fluffy. Fold in the coffee
and chopped nuts.

2 Spoon the mixture into the paper
cases. Bake for 15 minutes, or until
risen and firm to the touch.

3 While the cakes are in the oven,
make the syrup. Dissolve the sugar in
the espresso coffee.

4 As soon as the cakes come out of the
oven, pierce them in several places
with a skewer and drizzle the coffee
syrup over the top. Leave to cool.

5 To make the topping, melt the
chocolate in a heatproof bowl over a
pan of gently simmering water, then
leave to cool slightly.

6 Whisk the mascarpone and melted
chocolate together until smooth. Spread
over the cakes, decorate each with a
walnut half and serve immediately.

PER SERVING: Energy 339kcal/1414kJ; Protein 5.4g; Carbohydrate 33.9g, of which sugars 22.7g; Fat 21.1g, of which saturates 10.3g; Cholesterol 86mg; Calcium 56mg; Fibre 0.7g; Sodium 134mg.

Serves 10

1 large navel orange, unpeeled
350g/12oz/3 cups ground almonds
300g/11oz/generous1½ cups caster
   (superfine) sugar
115g/4oz/1 cup plain (all-purpose) flour
5ml/1 tsp baking powder
150g/5oz/10 tbsp butter, cubed,
   plus extra for greasing
6 eggs
2 pomegranates, seeds only

For the syrup

250ml/8fl oz/1 cup pomegranate juice
60ml/4 tbsp clear honey
15ml/1 tbsp pomegranate molasses

Almond and Orange Cake

This is a modern variation on a classic almond cake. Both Bulgaria and Romania have abundant almond crops, and almonds often appear in their recipes.

1 Grease a 15cm/6in square baking tin (pan) with butter, and line with baking parchment.

2 Put all the ingredients for the syrup in a pan and stir well over medium heat until the honey has dissolved. Cook, stirring, for 10–12 minutes, or until the liquid has a syrupy consistency.

3 Put the whole orange in a small pan, cover with water and boil for 25 minutes, or until the skin is soft. Remove and cool. Put the whole orange in a food processor or blender and process to a purée. Set aside.

4 Preheat the oven to 180°C/350°F/Gas 4. Put the ground almonds into a mixing bowl and add half the sugar, the flour and the baking powder. Mix well.

5 Beat the remaining sugar with the butter cubes until light and creamy. Add the eggs one at a time, beating well after each addition. Add the puréed orange and mix well.

6 Gradually fold in the almond mixture and pour this into the prepared baking tin. Bake for 50–60 minutes. Test to see if it's fully cooked by inserting a skewer; the cake is ready if the skewer comes out clean. When cooked, remove from the oven and leave to cool slightly before turning it out on to a rack to cool completely.

7 Using a skewer, make deep holes in the top of the cake and slowly pour over the syrup, which will soak into the cake. Pile the pomegranate seeds on top, and serve.

PER SERVING: Energy 569kcal/2381kJ; Protein 13g; Carbohydrate 53.5g, of which sugars 41.1g; Fat 35.4g, of which saturates 10.7g; Cholesterol 149mg; Calcium 148mg; Fibre 3.3g; Sodium 163mg.

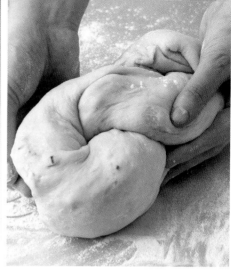

Romanian Babka

Babka is a sweet yeast cake from Russia and Poland, with versions throughout Eastern Europe, including the Romanian interpretation, cozonac. Recipes always include a fruit filling, often with raisins. This version combines chocolate with fresh cherries and has a crumbly almond topping.

Serves 10

For the almond topping

40g/1½oz/3 tbsp cold butter

50g/2oz/½ cup plain (all-purpose) flour

80g/3¼oz/scant ½ cup caster (superfine) sugar

100 almonds, coarsely chopped

For the loaf

10g/¼oz dried yeast

90ml/6 tbsp warm milk

1 large egg

1 small egg yolk

50g/2oz/¼ cup caster (superfine) sugar

200g/7oz/scant 2 cups plain (all-purpose) flour

50g/2oz/¼ cup unsalted (sweet) butter, softened and cubed

300g/11oz dark chocolate, minimum 70 per cent cocoa solids, coarsely grated

300g/11oz fresh cherries, halved and pitted

1 egg yolk, beaten

SERVING SUGGESTION

This cake is delicious when served with a creamy mascarpone.

1 For the almond topping, place the butter, flour and sugar in a food processor and process until the mixture resembles chunky breadcrumbs. Mix in the almonds to achieve a crumbly consistency. Chill in the refrigerator.

2 Put the dried yeast in a bowl with the warm milk, stirring continuously to dissolve. In a separate bowl whisk the egg, egg yolk and the caster sugar for 2–3 minutes until creamy and pale in colour. Stir in the yeast mixture.

3 Put the flour in a large bowl and make a well in the centre. Pour in the egg and yeast mixture, pulling everything together to form a dough. Add the butter and knead for at least 10 minutes until the dough is smooth. Place the dough in a large greased bowl, cover with a cloth and leave to rise for 2 hours in a warm place.

4 Preheat the oven to 180°C/350°F/Gas 4. Butter and line a loaf tin (pan) with baking parchment and then butter the parchment. Place the grated chocolate and prepared cherries in a bowl. Roll the dough into a square about 1cm/½in thick on a well-floured surface. Brush the edges with egg yolk and spread all but 30ml/2tbsp of the chocolate and cherry filling on to the rolled dough.

5 Roll up the dough from one side into a tight log shape, pinching the ends to seal. Twist in four or five places along the log to create a horseshoe shape, then cross the two halves over each other to form an open-ended figure of eight; twist again and fit into the prepared loaf tin. The aim is to get a plaited look.

6 Spread the top with the remaining chocolate and cherry filling. Sprinkle with the almond topping and leave covered in a warm place for about 1 hour until doubled in volume.

7 Bake the babka for 1 hour and 20 minutes until cooked. Leave in the tin for a few minutes and then transfer to a wire rack to cool.

PER SERVING: Energy 430.5kcal/1805.3kJ; Protein 6.8g; Carbohydrate 57g, of which sugars 36g; Fat 21.2g, of which saturates 11g; Cholesterol 87mg; Calcium 89mg; Fibre 1.4g; Sodium 89mg.

Useful addresses

AUSTRALIA
Food shops and markets
Bosnus Convenience Store
5/107 Turpin Road
Labrador
4215 Gold Coast
Tel: 07 5528 4872
www.bosnusconvenience.com

Polka Deli
22 Post Office Place, Glenroy,
VIC 3046
Tel: 03 9304 4700
www.polka.net.au.about.html

Restaurants
Transylvania Winery and
  Restaurant
Monaro Highway
Cooma
New South Wales 2630
Tel: 02 6452 4374

CANADA
Food shops and markets
Quality European Deli
1390 Walker Road
Windsor, Ontario
Tel: (519) 252 8243

Bucharest European Deli
1277 York Mills Road
Parkwoods Plaza
Toronto, Ontario
Tel: (416) 429 8379
www.bucharestdeli.com

Restaurants
La Maison Rustik
5461, Rue Sherbrooke Ouest
Montreal, Quebec
Tel: (514) 487 9990
lamaisonrustik.host56.com

Moldova Restaurant
5000 Dufferin Street, Unit 1
Toronto, ON M3H 5T5
Tel: (416) 665 4566
www.moldovarestaurant.com

The Old House
430 West Pender, Vancouver, BC
Tel: (604) 569 1883
www.theoldhouse.ca

Acacia Bistro & Import Ltd.
1103 Denman St.
Vancouver, BC
Tel: (604) 633 3885

UNITED KINGDOM
Food shops and markets
RoExport
Romanian Cultural Centre
Manchester Square
18 Fitzhardinge Street
London W1H 6EQ
Tel: 020 7486 0295
sales@roexport.co.uk

Rozova Dolina
11 Garman Road
Tottenham, London N17 0UR
Tel: 020 8885 4777

Patisserie La Romana
33 Burnt Oak Broadway
London HA8 5JZ
Tel: 020 8205 0004

Karlovo
Unit 8, Abbey Park Industrial
  Estate
Abbey Road, Barking
Essex IG11 7BT
Tel: 020 8591 7898

Prahova
652 Kingsbury Road
Kingsbury, London NW9 9HN
Tel: 07817 413649

Romania Food Centre
198 Station Road
Edgware, London HA8 7AR
Tel: 020 8958 4442

Restaurants
The Romanian Restaurant
32 Old Bailey
St Pauls, London EC4M 7HS
Tel: 08721 482199

Restaurant Valentine
333 Green Lanes
London N4 1DZ
Tel: 020 8800 1777

Restaurant Arda 2
156A Seven Sisters Road
London N7 7PL
Tel: 020 7263 5902

The Britannia
2 Sebastopol Road
Edmonton
London N9 0QH
Tel: 0208 803 8409

USA
Food shops and markets
A & M International Food
  Market
1916 Welsh Road
Philadelphia, PA 19115
Tel: (215) 969 1610

Zeytinz
24 West 40th Street
New York, NY 10018
Tel: (212) 575 8080
www.zeytinz.com

Indo-European Foods Inc.
1000 Air Way
Glendale, CA 91201
Tel: (818) 247 1000
www.indo-euro.com

Sunnyside Meat Market
3–10 43rd Street, Queens
New York NY 11104
Tel: (718) 615 1011

Taste of Europe: Romanian-
  Hungarian Bakery
1811 Wiley St, Hollywood
Miami, FL 33020
Tel: (954) 922 7345

Beograd Meat Market
2933–39 West Irving Park Road
Northwest Side, Chicago, IL
Tel: (773) 478 7575

Romanian Kosher
7200 N Clark St, Chicago
IL 60626
Tel: (773) 761 4141

Restaurants
Bistro Metro Restaurant
10721 Metropolitan Ave
Flushing, NY 11375
Tel: (718) 263 5444

Mignon's Romanian
  Restaurant
1253 Vine St, Los Angeles
CA 90038
Tel: (213) 461 4192

J & R's Smokehouse
1420 Jacobsburg Road
Wind Gap, PA 18091
Tel: (610) 863 6162

Danube
1303 Westwood Blvd.
Los Angeles, CA 90024
Tel: (310) 473 2141

Old Europe
1209 East Carson St.
Pittsburgh, PA 15203
Tel: (412) 488 1700

Dunarea Restaurant
821 N Euclid, Unit # C
Anaheim, CA 92801
Tel: (714) 772 7233

Romanian Garden
Outer Boroughs
4604 Skillman Ave
Queens, NY 11104
Tel: (718) 786 7894

Restaurant Bulgaria
4724 W Lawrence
Chicago, IL 60630
Tel: (773) 282 0300

**ADVICE ON FISH
SUSTAINABILITY**

The Environmental Defense Fund
257 Park Avenue South
New York, NY 10010
Tel: (800) 684-3322
www.edf.org

World Wildlife Fund
Tel: +41 22 364 91 11
www.panda.org

Index

Publisher's acknowledgements
The publishers would like to thank the
following for permission to reproduce their
images: p6 Peter Adams/Corbis;
p7l Caroline Penn/Imagestate/Photolibrary;
p7r Gavriel Jecan/Corbis; p8t Richard
Nebesky/Robert Harding Picture Library
Ltd/Alamy; p8bl The Photolibrary Wales/
Alamy; p8br Gregory Wrona/Alamy;
p9t Richard Bickel/Corbis; p10 private
collection/Archives Charmet/The
Bridgeman Art Library; p11tl The Print
Collector/Alamy; p11tr Antoine Gyori/
Corbis Sygma; p11b The Art Gallery
Collection/Alamy; p12l Ace Stock Limited/
Alamy; p12r Alan King/Alamy; p13l Vassil
Donev/epa/Corbis; p13r Robert Ghement/
epa/Corbis; p14l Bogdan Cristel/Reuters/
Corbis; p14r Petrut Calinescu/Alamy;
p15tl Grapheast/Alamy; p15tr Biosphoto/
Gunther Michel/Still Pictures; p15b
Photolibrary; p16t Leila Cutler/Alamy;
Gregory Wrona/Alamy; p17t Moreleaze
Travel London/Alamy; p21r Kristen
Soper/Alamy. t=top, b=bottom, r=right,
l=left, m=middle. All other photographs
© Anness Publishing Ltd.